EASY
Animal Carvings

Simple, Stylized, Step-by-Step
Wolves, Whales, Birds, Bears, and More

Wouter de Bruijn

© 2024 by Wouter de Bruijn and Fox Chapel Publishing
Company, Inc.

Easy Animal Carvings is an original work, first published in 2024
by Fox Chapel Publishing Company, Inc. The patterns contained
herein are copyrighted by the author. Readers may make copies
of these patterns for personal use. The patterns themselves,
however, are not to be duplicated for resale or distribution
under any circumstances. Any such copying is a violation of
copyright law.

ISBN 978-1-4971-0479-2

The Cataloging-in-Publication Data is on file with the
Library of Congress.

Managing Editor: Gretchen Bacon

Acquisitions Editor: Kaylee J. Schofield

Editor: Joseph Borden

Designer: Mike Deppen

Proofreader: Kurt Connelly

Indexer: Jay Kreider

To learn more about the other great books from Fox Chapel
Publishing, or to find a retailer near you, call toll-free
800-457-9112 , reach us by mail at 903 Square Street, Mount Joy,
PA 17552 or visit us at *www.FoxChapelPublishing.com*.

We are always looking for talented authors. To submit an idea,
please send a brief inquiry to
acquisitions@foxchapelpublishing.com.

Printed in China
First printing

Introduction

Like many woodcarvers, my first steps into woodcarving started with a wooden spoon. I took a spoon carving workshop while on holiday in Norway. At the end of the workshop, I had a sore hand and a lump of wood that vaguely resembled a spoon. It took many more hours at home before I could call it a finished spoon. My first memories of woodcarving, however, are from seeing my grandfather at work creating many different types of carvings—from relief carving to stylized animals. One of the foxes you see below is a fox he made; the other one is a fox I carved, and one you can make too, as it is one of the 14 animals featured in this book.

The animals in this book range from a tiny wren to a great, big humpback whale (don't worry, it's not life-size!) and anything in between. The style of my carvings can best be described as a stylized version of the real animal. Rather than focusing on all the tiny details, I try to look at the bigger picture and pay more attention to the shape. This will sometimes require a bit of imagination to get the animal right, for example with the barn owl and its face. My favorite project of the book has to be the bear. It was a good challenge to make and it was a joy to see it come alive during the process. It became a stunning piece, and it has the presence and weight of a real bear.

Many carvings will look amazing with a simple finish like oil or wax, but sometimes a carving requires a bit of color to really finish it off. Painting can be intimidating at first, but try to divide it by sections and focus on shapes before jumping to the smaller details. This will make it much easier to tackle a potentially difficult paint job. With many animals, a simple color-scheme will work just as well as a very detailed paint job. And with a stylized design, like the designs in this book, a stylized paint job will look much better than one that is too detailed.

I hope that the projects in this book will help you get your animal carvings to the next level, give you the confidence to paint your carvings, and give you a sense of how to create your own designs. Above all, I hope you'll enjoy making the animals in this book, either for yourself or as a gift for someone else.

WdsBruijn

Table of Contents

28

67

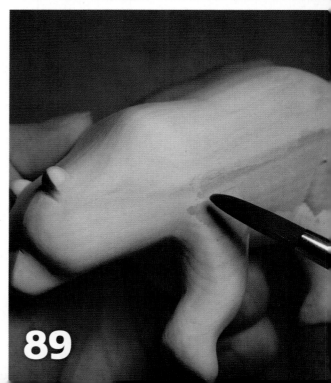

89

44

49

73

80

111

Getting Started

If you're new to carving, there are a few things you should keep in mind before you begin. In this chapter, we will discuss some woodcarving basics, such as using knives, gouges, and saws, various woods and their properties, essential safety considerations, and finishing and painting your projects. Once you've familiarized yourself with these concepts, you'll be ready to tackle any project in this book!

USING YOUR TOOLS

Using your woodcarving tools in the correct way makes the process of woodcarving much safer and more enjoyable. Here, I will outline the best practices for the tools used in these projects. Consult each project for the specific tools you'll need.

KNIVES

There are several ways of holding a knife. However you hold it, it should feel comfortable to you. My preferred grip is a "thumb push grip," in which you use the thumb of your noncarving hand to push against the back of the blade. This gives you a lot of control, as you can only carve as far as your thumb can reach. This motion is often called a push cut.

You can also use the thumb of your carving hand to "pull" the knife toward you. In this instance, your thumb acts like a kind of anchor and you pull the knife

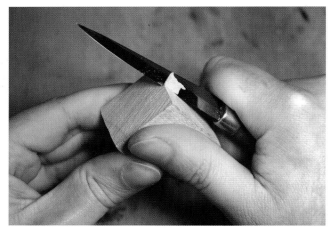

With a pull cut, you use your thumb as an anchor and pull the knife toward you.

toward you with your fingers. When doing this, make sure your thumb isn't in the way of the blade or wear some form of protection on the thumb of the hand holding the knife. This technique is called a pull cut.

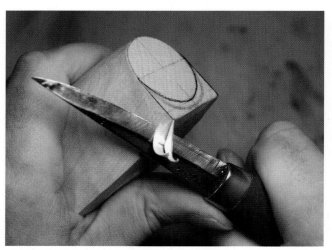

A push cut uses the thumb of the noncarving hand to push the blade forward.

For certain long-bladed knives, it can be useful to choke up on the blade as pictured above for detail cuts.

When you're using a knife with a long blade, like the Mora 106, it can be tricky to work on small details if you hold the knife like you normally would. You can make working on small details much easier by choking up on the knife, which basically means you're holding the knife on the blade. When using this grip, make sure you don't put your fingers on the cutting edge. Having big hands is beneficial with this grip; I can hold the blade with three fingers and grip the handle with my ring finger and pinky. This grip reduces the length of the knife, making your movements smaller and more precise, which is perfect for working on details like a bird's beak or the ears on a bear.

When holding a palm gouge correctly, the handle should be nestled in your palm as pictured above, right.

GOUGES

I prefer using a small palm gouge over a big gouge, especially when working on small details. The compact size of the palm gouge gives you more control than with a long-handled gouge. When working with a gouge, I always try to press down on the blade/shaft with a finger of my noncarving hand. I do this to steady the gouge and make sure I don't slip and accidentally cut away something I didn't mean to cut.

SAWS

I'm sure you've heard the advice "let the saw do the work." It's very sound advice. The less pressure you put on your saw, the straighter you will saw. Put too much pressure on it and you might end up with a cut that starts to curve, which will make the saw blade get stuck.

As the name suggests, a pull saw cuts when you pull it back toward you, as opposed a traditional saw that cuts when you push it away from you. Because it saws when you pull it back, it has a much thinner blade. This will cause less waste, which is nice, but it

A pull saw cuts when you pull the blade toward you.

can also cause your cut to wander. When you use too much pressure, the blade might curve, and you'll end up with a cut that isn't straight. I'm right-handed, and if I use too much pressure, my cuts drift to the left. When starting to cut a blank for your new project, keep in mind where the cut might drift.

One major advantage to a pull saw is that if you live somewhere with noise restrictions, or don't have the space or means for large power saws, the pull saw will help you prepare carving stock quietly and with limited space. Pull saws are also significantly cheaper than their powered counterparts. Whatever type of saw you use, always make sure the piece of wood you're sawing is fastened properly. Either clamp it down on your workbench or put it in a vise. When you use a vise, make sure the piece of wood is level; you can check this with a level or a level app on your phone (though the apps aren't always accurate).

The saw I use has two sides. One side has bigger, coarse teeth, which are used when cutting along the grain. The other side has smaller teeth. This side is used when cutting across the grain. If I use the wrong side, the sawing takes much longer. I recommend getting a saw like this if you don't already have one.

STROPPING AND SHARPENING

Keeping your knife sharp will make carving both easier and safer. Carving with a dull knife will make you put more force on the knife, which could cause your hands to cramp up. It also increases the risk of the knife slipping and causing a nasty cut. There are many techniques to keep your tools sharp; in this section, I'll give an overview of my preferred practices.

STROPPING KNIVES

It's easier to keep a sharp knife sharp than to let it dull significantly and then resharpen it. You can do this by regularly stropping your blade. I use a leather strop with a stropping compound. Before I start carving, I strop both sides of my knife 50 times, for a total of 100 times. When I'm carving, I try to strop my knife every half hour or so. This time, I only do 10 to 15 strokes on each side. When working on small details, like a beak, I make sure to strop before starting to carve those details.

To strop your knife, first apply a stropping compound to your leather strop. Next, make smooth,

Small teeth (top) are good for cutting across the grain. Large teeth (bottom) are great at cutting along the grain.

Strop your knife by first applying a stropping compound to your leather. Then, pull the blade across the leather in a series of strokes that travel away from the cutting edge.

even strokes along the strop, pulling the knife away from, not toward, the cutting edge. Make sure the bevel is placed completely flat on the strop, and lift it up straight at the end of the strop. This is to avoid rolling the edge, which will dull the blade.

SHARPENING KNIVES

If you keep your knife sharp by regularly stropping it, sharpening it with a stone usually isn't needed at all. Only sharpen it when you break or chip the blade. There are several different ways of sharpening a knife. I prefer using a Belgian coticule stone, a natural whetstone, and I'll outline that process below.

To sharpen a knife with a whetstone, first place the stone on a wet tea towel or nonslip mat. Place the knife on top of the stone with the blade edge pointing toward you. Now pull the knife in the direction of the cutting edge, always making sure the bevel is touching

Stropping Tips

- Avoid putting too much pressure on your knife as you strop.
- Move your knife away from the cutting edge. If you move it toward the cutting edge (like you do when you're carving or sharpening), you risk dulling the blade and damaging your strop.
- When you have a curved knife, like the Morakniv 106, make sure to lift the handle a little bit so you also strop the tip of the knife.
- If you see the strop changing color, from the color of your compound to a dark gray, it means it's working.

To sharpen your knife with a whetstone, make a series of passes on each side of the blade, pulling the blade across the stone toward the cutting edge.

Sharpening Tips

If you have chips in your knife or it is very blunt, you may want to use a coarser stone or pull the knife over the stone more than 10 times per side.

You can test the sharpness of your knife by cutting across the grain of a piece of basswood. You should get a smooth cut, and when the light hits it at the right angle, it will reflect the light a bit. If your knife isn't sharp, you'll get a sort of "fuzzy" finish. Or, if you have chipped your knife, you'll see a mark on the cut you've made, a line where the chip is.

the stone. Repeat this roughly 10 times. Finally, switch to the other side and repeat.

STROPPING GOUGES

Stropping a gouge looks a little different than stropping a knife. To hone the inside, I have a small stropping block, made by Flexcut, which has several ridges on it. These ridges are shaped like the inside "curve" of the gouge.

Just as with stropping a knife, put some stropping compound on the strop and move the gouge over the strop. Hold the gouge at an angle—for my gouges this is 20 degrees—and pull the gouge over the strop. If you don't have a stropping block, you can also use a dowel or other piece of wood that fits the contour of the gouge. Use a fine-grit sandpaper or emery cloth and wrap this around the dowel. When doing this, you don't need a stropping compound. To hone the outside bevel, you can switch to the flat strop you used for the knife, making sure to rotate the gouge gently so that every part of the bevel is equally honed.

SHARPENING GOUGES

Like with knives, if you keep your gouges properly stropped, you won't have need to regularly sharpen them.

I have only once sharpened a gouge, which was when it was chipped. To sharpen a gouge, I use different grits of sandpaper, starting at 150 grit and gradually working up through 320, 600, 1,200, and 2,000.

Put the sandpaper on a flat surface and, holding the gouge at the correct angle, pull it backward over the sandpaper. Keep sanding with 150 grit until the chip is gone and you have a straight edge again. Then, work your way up through the different grits. The final step is to sand the inside gouge, which is just like stropping it.

Stropping a gouge is similar to stropping a knife except you will need to use a strop that fits inside the curved blade.

CHOOSING WOOD

There are many types of wood, and some are easier to carve than others. All the projects in this book use basswood, which is especially great for entry-level carvers. In this section, I'll go over a few of the most common woods for small carvings such as these.

BASSWOOD

Basswood is considered a hardwood but is soft enough to carve easily. When it gets really dry, however, it becomes a lot tougher to work with. If it's very dry and your tools aren't sharp enough, the wood will feel a bit spongy to carve. If this happens, you'll have to sharpen your tools. You can also let the basswood soak in some hot water for a while. This will make it easier to work with.

Basswood is widely regarded as a great choice for beginning carvers. It's soft and has a beautiful grain pattern, and it is widely available in stores.

It's a very uniform wood, and although it is not the most exciting wood out there, sometimes the grain can surprise you and show its beauty when you finish a piece with oil. It also takes paint well, so is a great candidate if you plan to paint your finished piece.

OTHER WOODS

In this book, I only use one different type of wood: walnut. Walnut is a much harder wood than

Avoid Dry Ends

I buy my basswood in large blocks, which sometimes have very dry ends. If you find the same thing in the wood you buy, I advise cutting off the dry ends, as these are difficult to carve.

basswood and has a darker color. Combining the two woods gives a nice contrast between the pale basswood and the richness of the walnut.

Another easy-to-carve wood is butternut, also known as white walnut. This wood has roughly the same hardness as basswood, but it has a darker and richer color. This makes it ideal for finishing with oil.

You could also try cherrywood. Like other fruit woods, it can have gorgeous colors in the heartwood, and the grain looks amazing when finished with a simple oil. I would never finish a fruitwood with paint. Cherrywood is easiest to carve when it's still green. When it has dried, it'll become much harder.

Walnut's rich, dark color contrasts nicely with basswood.

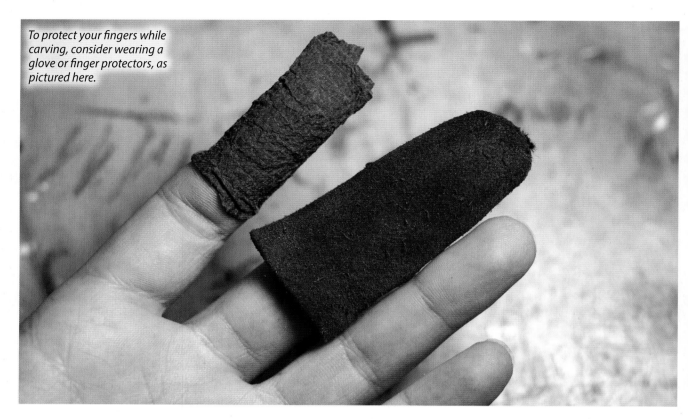

To protect your fingers while carving, consider wearing a glove or finger protectors, as pictured here.

SAFETY

Nobody likes getting hurt, so it's important to always think about your safety. Remember, danger doesn't take a day off! There are several ways to make carving a safer hobby, from wearing a simple glove to using safety glasses when using power tools. In this section, we'll go over some of the most essential tips to make your carving experience as safe as possible.

GEAR

Many carvers advise wearing a glove on the noncarving hand while carving. A thick, leather glove is great. One made of Kevlar is even better, as these offer great protection against slicing. No glove can fully protect against punctures, though.

The downside of wearing a glove is that you can get rather hot and sweaty hands, and you don't feel as much of the wood's character as you would with a bare hand. I prefer using either a small leather finger protector for my left thumb and left index finger (these are the fingers that are nicked most often) or

wrap them in a safety tape. Using these will give you more dexterity than using a glove. If you are quick to develop blisters on your carving hand, you can wear a cycling glove on that hand. This will give you some extra padding and they leave your fingers free.

Always use a mask when sanding, even when sanding outside. Getting dust stuck in your nose will make it feel like you have a permanent cold.

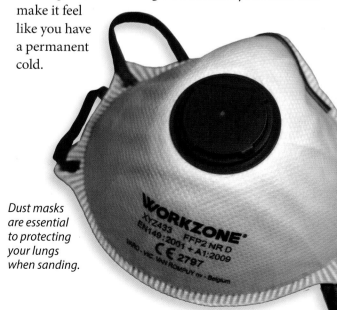

Dust masks are essential to protecting your lungs when sanding.

even carve a protector out of wood. Whatever it is, it's best practice to always put the tool back inside the protective cover after using it. This is to keep the tool from falling and getting damaged and to protect yourself and anyone that might venture into your carving space. Never try to catch a falling knife, gouge, or saw!

Here, you can see three examples of tool protectors and storage: a cut-resistant carrying case, a plastic cover, and a leather sheath.

My Pfeil gouges came in a basswood stand, both for protection and storage.

What's more, many woods contain toxins that are hazardous to inhale.

Make sure to replace the mask when it starts looking dirty. I prefer using an FFP2 or N95 mask; these will fit tightly against your face, creating a perfect seal. If you wear glasses, try getting a mask with a valve on it, as this will help prevent steamed-up glasses. You can also get masks or respirators with replaceable filters. These work the same as a normal dust mask but are just a bit bigger.

When using any power tool, wearing some form of eye protection is a wise thing to do. Spinning and cutting tools fling debris, which has an uncanny knack for honing in on a person's eyes. If you value your eyesight, safety glasses are a no-brainer.

STORING TOOLS SAFELY

Most tools come standard with some kind of protector. It could be a simple plastic sleeve or a fancy leather sheath. You can also make your own protector. For this, you can use cork, rubber, or you could

Additional Tips for Carving Safely

Make sure you're working in a well-lit area. Seeing what you're doing is always handy, even more so when using sharp tools. For some details in hard-to-see places, it can be useful to wear a headlamp. This will often be more effective than some lights on or around your workbench.

Never carve between your legs. The femoral arteries run through this area, and you don't want to hit those with your knife. If you want or need to support your wood piece on your leg, make sure to always cut away from yourself. You can also put a thick piece of leather or another hard-to-cut material atop your leg, if needed.

| 80 GRIT | 150 GRIT | 320 GRIT | 600 GRIT |

I recommend sanding your pieces with the sandpaper grits demonstrated above, beginning with the lowest grit.

SANDING

Sanding is often thought of as the most tedious and boring part of the entire process. Nonetheless, it's an important part of woodworking, so it's worth spending a good amount of time on. First, it should be noted that the higher the number identifying the sanding grit, the finer it is. The lower the number, the more material it removes when sanding. It's important to move up gradually through the different grits, as this will make sanding much faster. Switching to a finer grit too soon will prolong the time you spend sanding. A rough spot might be gone quickly with 80 grit but will take at least twice as long when you try to remove it with 150 grit.

If you start sanding with a very fine grit, such as 600, you'll be sanding for hours and hours (not to mention the amount of sandpaper you'll be using) before you see any results. I usually start my sanding process with an 80-grit sandpaper. This is a quick way to remove fairly large amounts of wood. You can also use this to get to some places that are hard to reach with your knife. With the 80 grit, I avoid small details like the beak of a bird. These small details are better saved for higher grits, as you don't want to remove too much too fast.

You'll notice a big difference in the look of the project after you've finished sanding with 80 grit. This is what you'll use to knock off any hard edges created while carving. Once you've finished sanding with this grit, your project should have a more refined shape that closely resembles what you expect the piece to look like when you're completely done.

From 80 grit, I go to 150 grit. With this, you can refine some details and it's safe to use on the small pieces, such as a bird's beak. You'll notice that sanding with 150 grit and above will take much less time when you compare it to sanding with 80 grit. That's because you're now in the refining stages, as opposed to bulk removal of material.

From 150, I move on to 320 grit. At first glance, this might look like a very fine sandpaper, but it can remove more wood than you might expect. You should be constantly checking your results as you sand. You can always remove more, but you can never remove less.

From 320, we move on to the final grit: 600. This will create a very smooth finish. For an even smoother finish, first sand it with 600 grit, then hold it under running water, getting the entire project wet. Pat it semi dry with a towel and let it dry completely. This will bring up all the wood fibers, which you can sand off with a final sanding with 600 grit. Wetting the project will also show any pen or pencil marks that you might've missed, and it gives you an idea of how the project will look when you finish it with oil.

After that, you're ready to apply a finish to your project. Keep in mind that some woods will not hold a finish as well if sanded to too high of a grit, and this is entirely dependent on the choice of wood and finish used. Experiment to find what achieves the results you want.

Sanding Tips

- For small projects, I like to use a rotary tool with a 120-grit sanding bit. You could also use a 60-grit sanding bit, but I find this much too coarse/aggressive. When using a rotary tool, don't use too high an RPM—10,000 is more than enough. Any RPM higher than that runs the risk of sanding away more than you intended.

- When the paper backing of the sandpaper becomes too flexible, it is time to get a new piece of sandpaper. Sometimes, you might be tempted to throw away all your used sandpaper. Saving a few pieces can be very useful. For example, a new piece of 150 grit may be too coarse and 320 a tad too fine. In that case, a used piece of 150 grit can be extremely useful.

- Before you start sanding with a new piece of sandpaper, pull it over the edge of your workbench (with the back against the workbench). This will make it easier to fold.

- You can easily remove the dust on the sandpaper by rubbing it against your pants or a piece of cloth you've dedicated for this; it will make your sandpaper last a bit longer.

- Try to always sand along the grain (especially with the finer grits), and end with one final pass in one direction for a smooth result.

- You don't have to use a lot of pressure while sanding; applying gentle pressure is more than enough.

- When switching from one grit to the next, remove all the dust before continuing. This will both show any spots you've missed and prevent your new piece of sandpaper getting full of dust. You can easily do this with either a microfiber cloth or vacuum cleaner, or by brushing it off with a normal brush. Also do this at the end of the sanding process. If you've drilled holes, make sure to remove the dust from there, too.

FINISHING YOUR WORK

To paint or not to paint, that's the question. Painting your project can completely transform it from a beautiful piece of work to a real eye catcher. You can also choose to finish pieces with wax (colored or clear), oil, or burnishing, letting the natural wood characteristics show through. You can also go for a mix, painting part of the project and applying oil to a different part. The options are nearly endless. Whichever finish you decide to use, test it on a piece of scrap wood first.

PAINT

It is easiest to start by drawing the design on the sanded wood. When you use a freshly sharpened pencil, you get thin lines which won't show up under the paint. This is especially useful when painting with lighter colors.

I prefer to finish my pieces with watercolors or acrylics, mineral oil, or a finishing wax. Each can produce a simple but stunning result.

I mainly use watercolor, which can take some getting used to. It's thinner than other paint, like acrylics, which can cause the paint to "bleed" or run, which means that it can flow beyond where you want it to go. If you don't want the colors to blend together, it is best to creep up to the line with your paintbrush. Do this by first painting a short distance away from the line and slowly getting closer. This lets the wood soak up the water and makes it less likely the paint will spread past the line. Using a brush with short hairs will also help prevent the paint bleeding because there will be less water on your brush.

I like the unpredictability of watercolor. It adds a more natural feel to the finished project. Every brushstroke will produce a slightly different finish, as the amount of paint or pigment differs every time. In general, it is best to paint the dark colors first, followed by the lighter colors. If a lighter color bleeds into a darker color, it is less noticeable than if it's the other way around.

Paint in thin layers and let the paint completely dry before deciding whether you want to apply a new layer. If you leave the paint as a thin layer or if you use a translucent paint (check the packaging to find out what type it is), you can still see the grain through it. If you apply a thicker layer, the grain won't be as visible, if visible at all.

Another popular paint to use is acrylic paint. It's a versatile paint, readily available and easy to paint with. You can use it straight from the tube or thin it with water or special thinners if you want to keep some of the wood grain visible.

OIL

A simple finish with a mineral oil, for example, will really make the grain stand out and give the project a natural look. After drying, the wood will turn slightly matte. You can apply oil with a brush or a cloth. Make sure to clean your brush well after use. Some oils are prone to spontaneous combustion. Read the manufacturer's instructions on cloth or towel disposal closely.

Another popular oil is Danish oil. It will give your piece a satin finish. It will also provide excellent

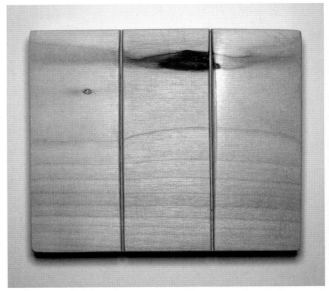

Each method of finishing creates a different reaction in the wood. Burnished wood is semi-glossy, oiled wood often has a high shine and vibrant woodgrain, and waxed wood typically has a somewhat glossy appearance.

protection against water. For a matte finish, you could also go for a lemon oil. This oil doesn't darken the wood and gives off a lovely, lemony smell. Lemon oil can be quite acidic, though, which may react poorly with some woods.

WAX

Many clear waxes will produce a glossy finish. These provide good protection, but don't allow the grain to stand out as much as it does with oil. Wax can be applied over watercolors, adding a richer tone. Before applying the wax over a layer of watercolor, make sure the paint has completely dried.

BURNISHING

Burnishing is a process in which you rub a hard object, such as plastic or wood, or a smooth rock, over the finished project. By rubbing vigorously, the friction between the two pieces creates heat and this burns off the dried, soft cells of the wood and exposes the harder cells. This produces a semi-glossy finish, a little less glossy than a wax finish.

Projects

Eurasian Wren

Not only does this tiny bird have a powerful voice, but it also has a unique look. The little upright tail will immediately identify it as a wren. By following the steps laid out here, you'll learn to make you own version of this popular bird.

TOOLS AND MATERIALS

- Sloyd knife (I use a Morakniv 106)
- A ⅛" (3mm) #11 gouge (I use a Pfeil 11/3)
- ¹⁄₁₆" (1.5mm) drill bit
- Pin vise, drill, or drill press
- Brushes
- Non-marring pliers
- Wire cutters
- Contact paper (or similar) and pen/pencil
- Basswood: 1¹⁄₁₆" x 1³⁄₁₆" x 1¾" (2.7 x 3 x 4.5cm)
- Sandpaper
- Aluminum wire, brown: ¹⁄₁₆" thick, 1³⁄₁₆" long (1.5 x 30mm)
- Base: a branch or a cork; something heavy enough that it won't topple over when the bird is standing on it
- Mineral oil

PAINTS

- Sepia watercolor (I use Winsor & Newton)
- Burnt umber watercolor (I use Winsor & Newton)
- Chinese white watercolor (I use Winsor & Newton)
- Gray watercolor (I use Payne's Gray by Winsor & Newton)
- Ivory black acrylic (I use Amsterdam Acrylic)

PROJECT PATTERN ON PAGE 121.

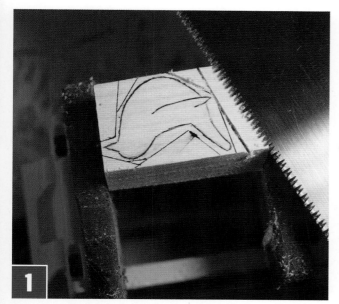

1

Copy the side view design to the wood with pen or pencil.
Orient it so the grain runs from beak to tail. You can copy the
design onto a thick piece of paper or cardboard and trace
around that, or you can use tracing or carbon paper. Make
sure the design is easy to see and saw as close to the lines
as possible.

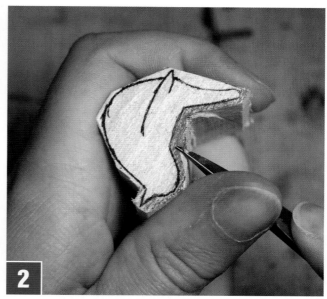

2

**Remove all the highlighted wood down the back of the
bird.** Take lots of care when you get to the beak. It's better to
leave a little too much wood. You'll be able to remove this in a
later stage of the process. For ease, draw a line down the front
of the beak. This way, you'll have a target to carve to.

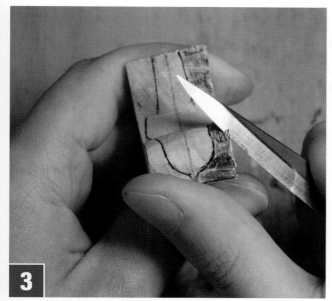

3

Draw the pattern on the back of the bird. Draw a line
down the middle of the bird. This will be useful when you start
rounding off the edges at a later stage. Start carving away all
the highlighted wood (this is the left side of the bird, the side
without the pattern on), leaving a little extra wood around
the beak.

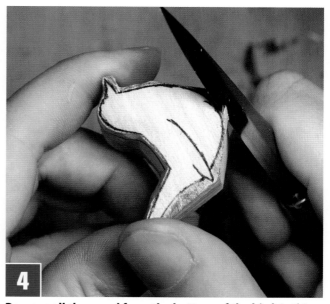

4

Remove all the wood from the bottom of the bird. In this
step, you must be careful of both the beak and the wing tips at
the back of the bird. For ease, draw a line across the bird where
the wing tips are, just like you did on the beak in Step 2. When
all the wood has been removed, draw a line down the middle
of the bird.

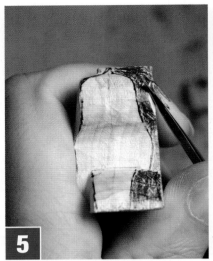

5

Remove all the highlighted wood. This is the from the side on which you drew the pattern at the start of the project. Redraw the pattern of the wings on both sides of the bird. This doesn't have to be perfectly symmetrical.

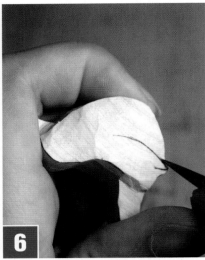

6

Using the very tip of your knife, score a line down the wings. Go from a very shallow cut at the base of the wing, gradually getting deeper toward the end of the wing.

7

Establish the bird's width. Just under the wing tips, measure ¼" (6mm) from each side of the center line. This will become the width of the bird. Make a mark and carve the sides down to this mark. You're doing this under the wings. You could also use a small gouge for this step, such as a ⅛" (3mm) #11.

8

Round off the edges. Working toward the center line, start cutting away the hard edges on the back, bottom, and head. You can leave the beak for the next step. When you're rounding off the edges, you'll notice that the wings will stand out less. To make sure they are still well defined, you'll have to work on them again, making the same cuts as in the previous step.

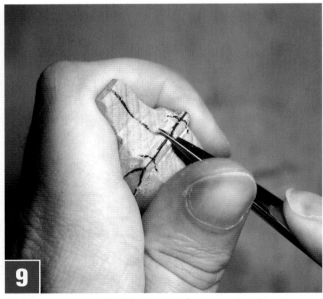

9

Remove any wood left between the two wingtips. You can do that either with a small gouge or your carving knife. If you're going to use your knife, make a stop cut at the edges of the wings. This will prevent you cutting them off accidentally.

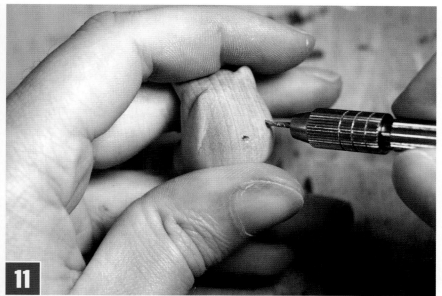

TIP: You can always use a bit of sandpaper to do the final bit of detailing on delicate pieces—150 grit should do the trick.

10

Carve the beak. Be careful to avoid cutting off the entire beak. Start by drawing the pattern on just the beak so you will have a guideline to carve to. Make sure your knife is very sharp, and avoid using too much pressure when making the cuts. Instead of removing a lot of wood at once, make several small cuts. When you have carved down to the line, start rounding off the beak. The wren has a narrow, conical beak. Recreating this exactly can be difficult, so a sturdier, triangular beak will also work.

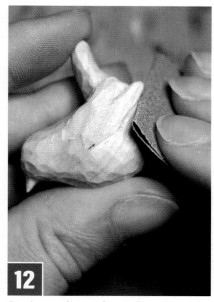

11

Mark the leg placement. Using the center line you drew on the bottom of the bird, mark where the legs will go. On the pattern, I've marked how far back they should roughly be. At that height, make two marks about ⅛" (3mm) from the center line. This will make the legs sit ¼" (6mm) from each other. Using an awl or the tip of your knife, create a couple of puncture marks. These will help you get your drill bit started. Now drill two, ⅜" (1cm)-deep holes at the angle you can see on the pattern. It doesn't have to be exactly at that angle; the aluminum legs can easily be adjusted.

12

Begin sanding. After drilling, you can sand the entire bird, starting with 80 grit. Don't use this on the delicate beak, as it will leave marks too deep.

13 **Sand with 150 grit.** Sand the entire bird again. With this, you can also sand the beak.

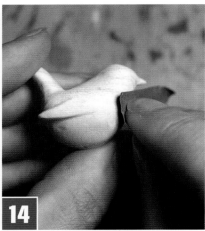

14 **Sand up through 600 grit.** After sanding the entire bird smooth with 150 grit, you can move on to 320 grit and eventually 600 grit. After sanding with 600 grit, hold the bird under running water. Let it dry, then sand it again with 600 grit. The running water will make the fibers stand up, making it easy to get an even smoother finish.

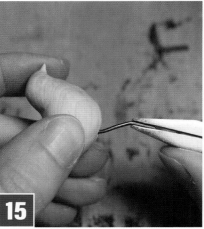

15 **Make the legs.** Cut two pieces of 1 ³⁄₁₆" (3cm)-long aluminum wire and press them into the bird. If you feel this is too tight, you can either redrill the holes or sand the top of the legs. This should make it easier to fit them. Using a non-marring pair of pliers, make a bend roughly ³⁄₈" (1cm) down from the bird. The lower part of the leg will go in the base, and you'll end up with a ³⁄₈" long leg.

16 **Affix the bird to a base and apply a finish.** Drill two holes in the base you want to use. These holes should be vertical and should also be about ³⁄₈" (1cm) deep. Make sure the base is heavy enough and doesn't fall over when you place the bird on it. The Eurasian Wren doesn't have the most exciting plumage, so this project looks great when finished with your oil of choice. If you want to paint your bird, start with a thin layer of a sepia watercolor—just enough to get a slightly darker base color. Then, stipple on darker colors like burnt umber and a less-diluted sepia. The chest is lighter, so that won't need as much work as the top parts. Paint the beak with a gray watercolor. For the eyes, use black acrylic. Finally, add some white highlights around the eyes, the "eyebrow" being the most important.

Clucking Chicken

A simple, but funny bird to carve. Make just one and put it in a bookcase or make several and you have the start of your very own farmyard. Wherever you place this bird, it will improve your day when you see it.

TOOLS AND MATERIALS

- Sloyd knife (I use a Morakniv 106)
- General purpose carving knife (I use Flexcut KN12)
- Saw
- Awl
- $\frac{1}{16}$" (1.5mm) drill bit
- Pin vise, drill, or drill press
- Brushes
- Pen
- Pencil
- Basswood: 1½" x 1³⁄₁₆" x ⅞" (3.8 x 3 x 2.3cm)
- Basswood: 2" x 2" x ⅜" (5 x 5 x 1cm). A little smaller is possible, too. Or bigger, if you want to place more chickens on 1 piece.
- Sandpaper
- Aluminum wire (x2): $\frac{1}{16}$" thick, ¾" long (1.5 x 20mm)

PAINTS

- Azo Yellow Deep acrylic paint (I use Van Gogh)
- Chinese White (I use Winsor & Newton)
- Sap Green (I use Winsor & Newton)
- Cadmium Yellow Hue (I use Winsor & Newton)
- Burnt Umber (I use Winsor & Newton)
- Cadmium Red Deep (I use Winsor & Newton)

PROJECT PATTERN ON PAGE 122.

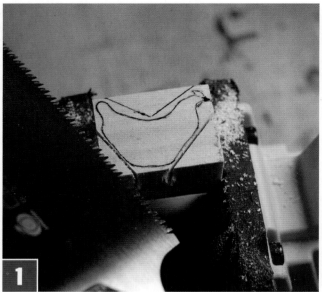

1

Copy the side view pattern on the block of wood. Make sure the grain runs from the front of the chicken down to the back. Use a saw to cut it out and saw as close to the lines as you can; this will reduce the work you need to do later on. Save one of the cutoffs. You can use this to test your finish on, whether that's oil or paint.

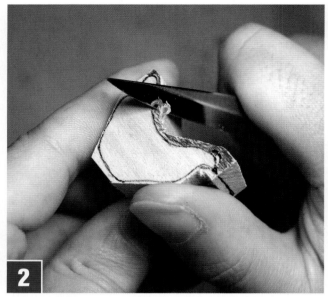

2

Remove all the highlighted wood down the back of the bird. When carving around the beak and comb, be careful to not carve away too much. Drawing a horizontal line across the beak will give you a guide to carve to.

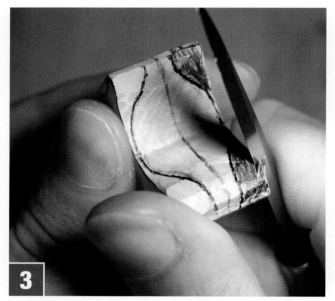

3

Draw a line down the center of the bird and draw the top view pattern on the back. The centerline will help you keep the carving symmetrical. Once done, begin removing all the highlighted wood.

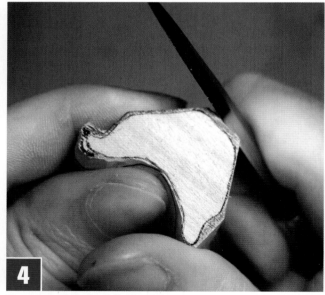

4

Remove all the highlighted wood down the front and bottom of the bird. When you can get to the beak and wattle (the part under the hen's throat, starting just behind the beak), make sure you don't accidentally carve away too much wood. You can refine this work later.

5 Remove the highlighted wood from the right side of the bird.** Just like you did on the back of the bird, draw a center line down the entire length of the bird. Then, remove the highlighted portions. This is the side on which you drew the pattern at the start of the project. When you hold up the project now, you should already start to see the shape of the chicken starting to emerge.

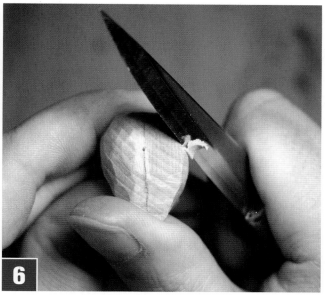

6 Start rounding off the edges.** Do this on both the top and the bottom of the bird. You can use the center line as a target to carve to. The chicken is a fairly rotund bird, so don't make it too round or narrow.

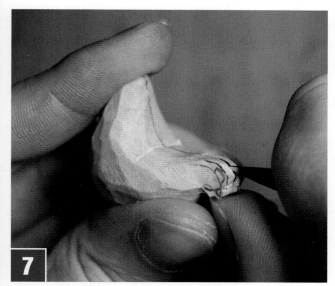

7 Redraw the pattern on the head.** Do this on both sides. Make a pen mark where you want the comb and wattle to go. Using the very tip of your knife, score a line just next to the comb and wattle. Carefully carve away the wood next to the comb and wattle. I have made mine the width of the pen mark I drew on the bird.

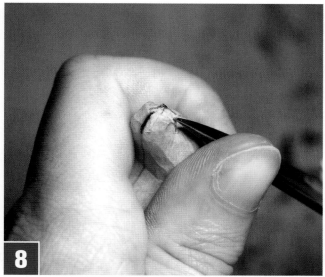

8 Begin carving the beak.** Draw a small triangle on top of where the beak will go. There should still be a bit of center line visible to help you locate the perfect place for that. Carefully carve away the wood on both sides of the beak. It will be a tiny beak, but it will stand out much more once painted. Now that you've carved the beak, comb and wattle, there will be some hard edges around the head. Round these off to create a smooth transition to the neck and beak.

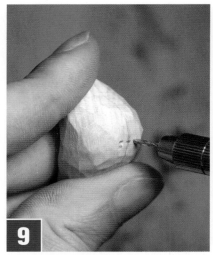 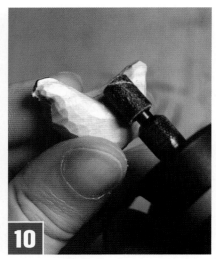 

Drill the leg holes. On the pattern, I've marked how far back the legs should be. Mark this place on the center line. Measuring from the center, make two marks ⅛" (3mm) from the center line. Using an awl or the tip of your knife, make two pilot holes for your drill to sit in. The holes should be roughly 9/32" (7mm) deep. Drill the holes vertically.

Begin sanding. The first stages can be done with a rotary tool with a 120-grit sanding bit (don't use anything coarser, and don't run your machine at speeds over 10,000 RPM). You could also sand by hand using a piece of 80-grit sandpaper. Both will get you the same result; the rotary tool will just get you there a bit faster. Don't use either option on the head; it is far too rough for the delicate features.

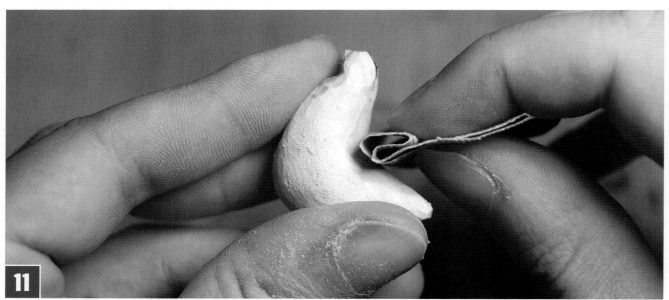

Continue sanding. Once you've completed sanding with the rotary tool or the 80-grit sandpaper, move on to 150 grit. With this, you can sand the head. Keep sanding with 150 grit until all marks from the previous sanding have been removed. Then, move on to 320 grit. Finish with a round of sanding with 600 grit. After sanding with 600 grit, hold the bird under running water, and after letting it dry, sand it again with 600 grit to get an even smoother surface.

Make the legs and base. Cut two pieces of aluminum wire, ¾" (2cm) long. Test to see if the legs fit in both the bird and the base. If they don't fit, sand them a bit until they do. Draw a circle on the piece of wood that will be used as the base. Use a saw to cut it out. Carve away the angles that are left. Slightly round off the edges at the top part of the base. Don't make this perfectly smooth. I've used a Flexcut KN12, but you can use your normal carving knife for this. Make two marks ¼" (6mm) away from each other, and drill two holes. This is where the chicken will stand. It looks more pleasing if you don't place the chicken precisely in the middle of the circle. Finally, use a coarse sandpaper or similar to rough up the top of the base. This gives the wood depth and will make the final paint job look livelier.

Paint the base. Use a green watercolor. Around the bottom edge of the base, paint a line of burnt umber watercolor. This doesn't have to be a very thick line; ⅛" (3mm) should be enough. Do this while the green paint is still wet. The brown and green paints will blend nicely, creating a natural transition between the brown ground and green grass.

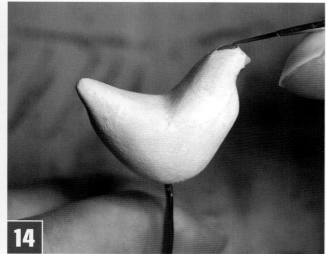

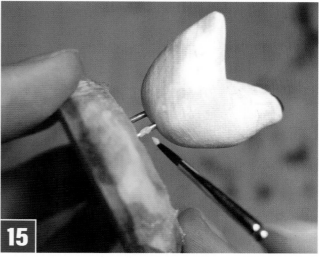

Paint the chicken. Chickens come in many different colors, but I've gone for a simple white chicken. Using a fairly big brush, paint the entire bird (apart from the head, comb and wattle) with a white watercolor (I used Chinese White by Winsor & Newton). It might need more than one coat of white paint to ensure the bird is uniformly covered. Wait for the paint to dry between each coat, and also wait before painting the beak and wattle. Using a thin brush, paint the beak with yellow. Paint the comb and wattle red. Make sure the paint isn't too wet, or else it will bleed into the parts you've painted white.

Paint the legs and attach the base. Give the middle bit of the legs, which will remain visible, a light sanding with 150-grit sandpaper. This is so the paint will stick better to the smooth, aluminum wire. Use a yellow acrylic paint, like Van Gogh Azo Yellow Deep, to paint the visible parts of the legs. I paint the legs when the chicken is on the base so I know how far I must paint. By doing this, you run the risk of accidentally getting some yellow paint on either the bird or the base, so don't rush and use as little paint as possible. You can touch up any unpainted parts after letting the paint dry and carefully removing the legs from the bird and base.

Waddling Mallard

A very cute addition to your carving repertoire, a duck. In this tutorial, you'll learn how to paint it to look like a male mallard, but you can finish it however you like. It's a friendly character and will cheer you up whenever you see it!

TOOLS AND MATERIALS

- Saw
- Sloyd knife (I use a Morakniv 106)
- Detail knife (I use a Flexcut KN19 Mini Pelican)
- A ⁵⁄₁₆" (8mm) #5 gouge (I use a Pfeil L 5/8)
- A ³⁄₁₆" (5mm) #9 gouge (I use a Pfeil L 9/5)
- A ⅛" (3mm) #11 gouge (I use a Pfeil L 11/3)
- ¹⁄₃₂" (1mm) drill bit and pin vise
- ⁵⁄₃₂" (4mm) drill bit and drill or drill press
- Paintbrushes
- Wire cutters
- Basswood: 1⁹⁄₁₆" x 3½" x 4 ⅛" (4 x 9 x 10.5cm)
- Basswood (x2): ¾" x ¾" x ³⁄₁₆" (20 x 20 x 5mm)
- Basswood (x2): ³⁄₁₆" x ¾" x ¾" (5 x 20 x 20mm); grain running lengthwise
- Sandpaper: 80, 150, 320 and 600 grit
- Copper wire (x2): ¹⁄₃₂" (1mm), ¼" (6mm) long
- Wood glue

PAINTS

- White watercolor (I use Winsor & Newton Chinese White)
- Neutral tint watercolor (I use Winsor & Newton)
- Yellow ochre watercolor (I use Winsor & Newton)
- Burnt umber watercolor (I use Winsor & Newton)
- Blue watercolor (I use Winsor & Newton Indanthrene Blue)
- Spring green watercolor (I use Winsor & Newton Viridian Hue)
- Black watercolor (I use Winsor & Newton Ivory Black)
- Orange watercolor (I use Winsor & Newton Transparent Orange)

PROJECT PATTERN ON PAGE 123.

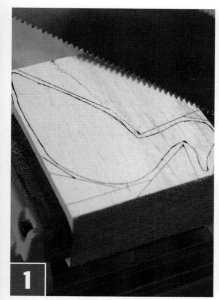

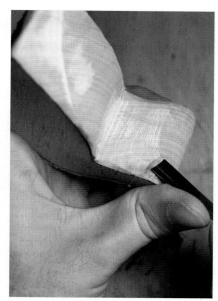

1

Copy and cut out the side view pattern. Copy the pattern onto the block of wood, with the grain running horizontally from chest to tail. Then, use a saw to cut it out, sawing as close to the lines as possible.

2

Remove all the highlighted wood down the back of the duck. For most of this, you can use your sloyd knife. On the back of the head and neck, I find it easier to use a small gouge to remove the wood. Use a gouge such as a ⁵⁄₁₆" (8mm) #5 gouge. Whichever tool you use, make sure you get a clean finish.

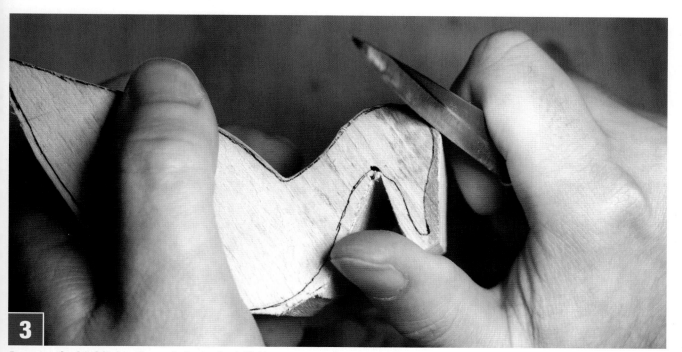

3

Remove the highlighted wood above the bill. You can use either your knife or a small gouge, such as a ⁵⁄₁₆" (8mm) #5 gouge. Make sure you don't carve beyond the line and accidentally make the bill too narrow.

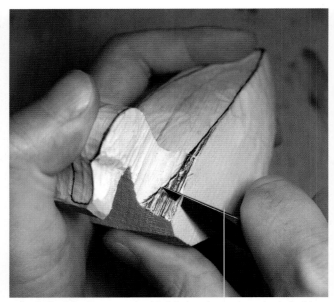

4

Copy the top view pattern onto the back of the duck and carve the left side. Remove the highlighted wood on the left side of the duck. This is the side without the main pattern on it. To remove the wood next to the head, it is easiest to use a small gouge, such as a ³⁄₁₆" (5mm) #9 gouge. Carve down toward the body, following the curve. A handy guide is provided on the main pattern. When you've removed the wood next to the head, remove the highlighted wood on the body. Follow the line of the body, gently curving toward the front of the neck.

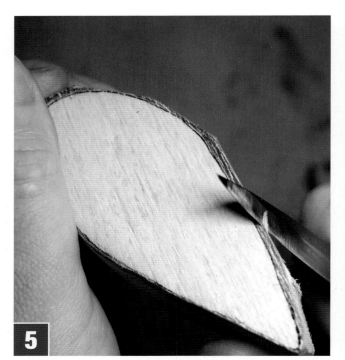

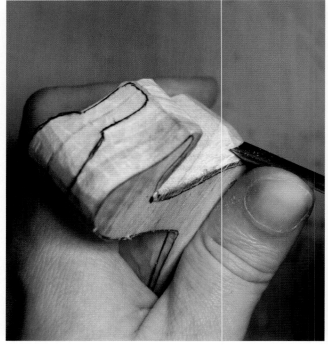

5

Remove all the highlighted wood on the underside of the duck. In front of the neck, switch to a small gouge, such as the ⁵⁄₁₆" (8mm) #5 gouge you used earlier. For the wood under the bill, switch back your knife and carve from the front of the bill back toward the body.

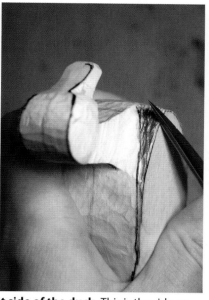

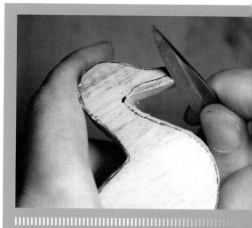

6

Remove the highlighted wood on the right side of the duck. This is the side on which you drew the main pattern at the start of the project. Remove the wood on the side of the head and neck with a small gouge, such as a ³⁄₁₆" (5mm) #9 gouge. Next to the neck, draw a line following the curve of the body, ending at the front of the neck. Remove all the highlighted wood on the outside of this line.

TIP: If you need to refine the shape of the bill (especially the top part), this is the time to do it, when you still have the main pattern as a guide. If you do refine it, make sure to redraw the pattern on top of the bill afterward.

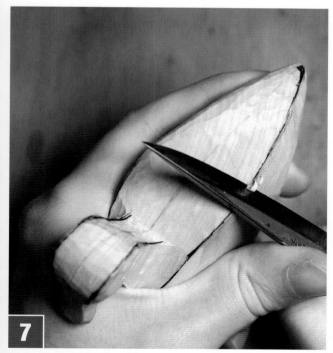

7

Round off the body of the duck. Make sure all the sides blend nicely. You will have to work on the area surrounding the neck some more after you've rounded that off in the next step.

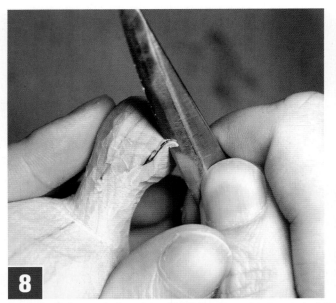

8

Round off the neck, head, and bill. Starting with the neck, followed by the head, and saving the bill until last. On top of the bill, follow the Y shape to get a bill that's narrow on top and flatter toward the end.

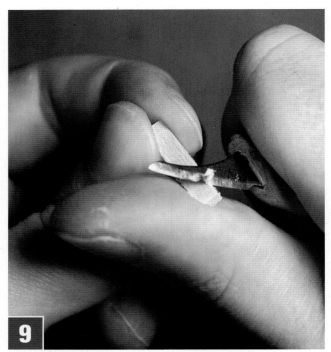

9

Begin carving the legs. With a small detail knife, round off a thin leg, getting it to a diameter of ⁵⁄₃₂" (4mm). It doesn't have to be perfectly round; it just has to fit snuggly in the hole you'll drill in the duck. To be extra safe, drill a test hole in a piece of scrap wood. The hole should be about ³⁄₈" (1cm) deep. Make two legs this way.

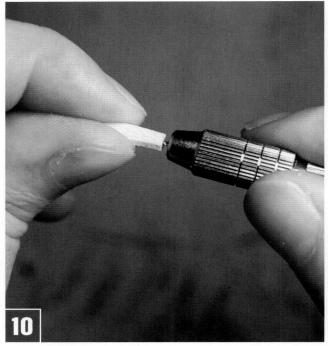

10

Create the linkage to the foot. Drill a ⅛" (3mm) deep hole in one end of each leg with a ¹⁄₃₂" (1mm) drill bit. Insert a ¼" (6mm)-long bit of copper wire in each. This side will connect to the foot/flipper.

11

Begin carving the feet. Copy the pattern of the foot/flipper onto a thin piece of basswood, with the grain running from the toes back to the heel. At the heel, drill a ⅛" (3mm) deep hole with a ¹⁄₃₂" (1mm) drill bit. Remove the highlighted wood. Follow the same process for a second foot.

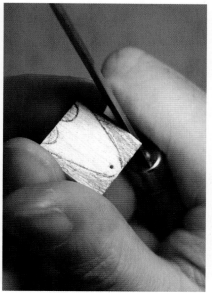

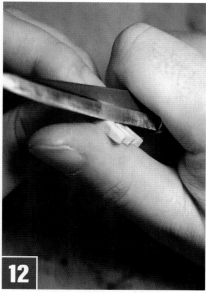

12

Narrow down the front of the foot and round off the edges. Don't round off the heels too much. If you do, the duck might have a tendency to fall over backwards.

13

Carve between the toes. With a small gouge, such as a ⅛" (3mm) #11, carve away some wood between the toes.

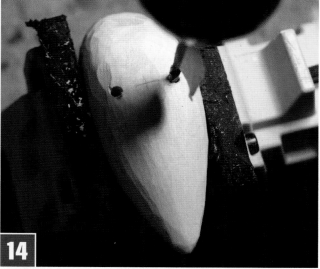

14

Drill holes in the bottom of the duck. These should be about ⅜" (1cm) deep and you should use the ⁵⁄₃₂" (4mm) drill bit. Try to drill them perfectly straight. On the pattern, I've marked where the legs are located. Find the middle of the bird and make a mark ⅜" to either side of this. This is where you should drill. Then, test fit the legs and feet. If the duck falls over backwards, you can remove wood from the tail or some from the bottom of the feet (toward the front) to make the duck lean forward slightly. Once you've found the proper balance point, mark the feet so you know which is right and which is left.

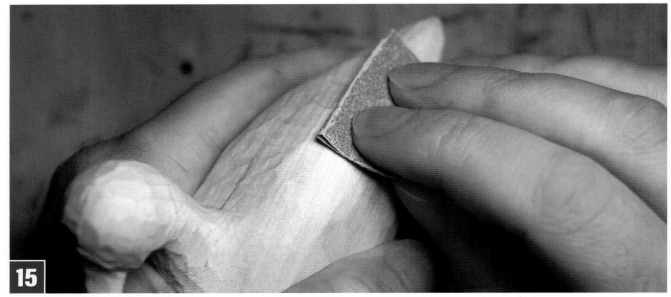

15

Start sanding the duck head and body. Begin with 80-grit sandpaper. Avoid sanding the bill with this paper. When you've sanded the entire duck (minus the bill), switch to 150 grit and sand the entire body, including the bill. When you sand the bill with this, only sand in one direction. Start at the top of the head and pull the sandpaper toward the end. This will give you much more control of how much you sand away. Then, move up to 320 grit followed by 600.

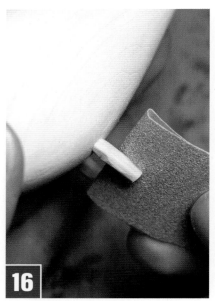

16

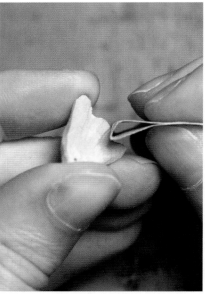

Sand the legs and feet. It is best to insert the legs before sanding them. Glue them in place by applying a small amount of wood glue inside the holes you've drilled. I've used a toothpick to do this. Start with 150 grit for these, gradually working your way up to 600. Don't sand the bottom of the feet too much, as they should remain as flat as possible. Once done, check the balance and make adjustments if needed.

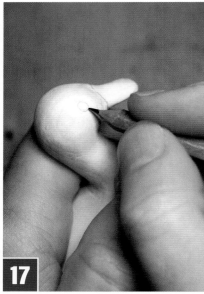

17

Draw the duck's features. Copy the design of the plumage onto the duck, trying to get it as symmetrical as possible. Using a freshly sharpened pencil is best for this, as it will allow you to get the thinnest lines possible.

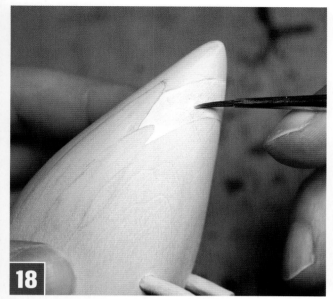

18

Begin painting. Start by painting the lightest parts: the white ring around its neck and the white patch at the end of the wings and tail. I use Winsor & Newton Chinese White watercolor for this, and to get a good finish, it will need at least two coats. Let the paint dry before moving on.

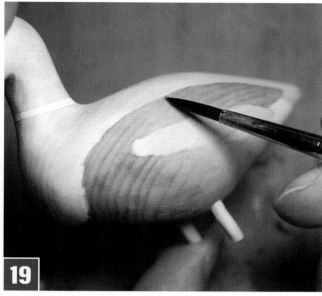

19

Paint the lower body. For the gray body, I use a thin coat of Winsor & Newton Neutral Tint watercolor. When you're applying this, it will look much darker because of the water.

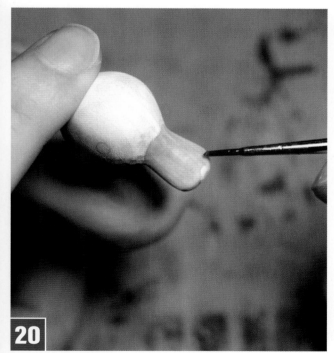

20

Paint the bill yellow. I use a thin layer of Winsor & Newton Yellow Ochre watercolor. Make sure the bill doesn't become too yellow.

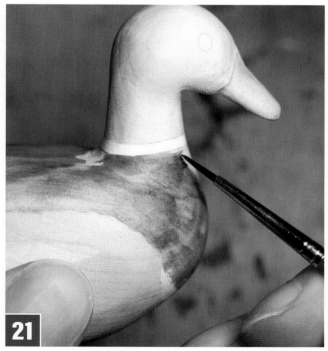

21

Paint the upper body. Next, paint the upper part of the body and chest with a burnt umber watercolor (I use Winsor & Newton). This doesn't have to be a completely even coat; a little bit of variation is perfect.

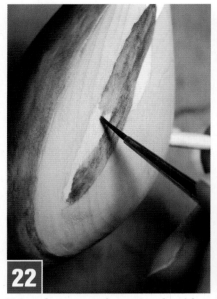

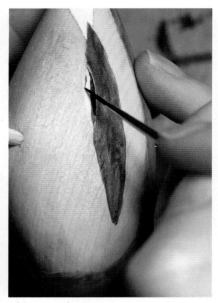

22

Using the same color, paint the sides. Give this more than one coat to get it a shade darker than the back and chest of the duck. Underneath the wings, there is a tiny blue patch. I've used Winsor & Newton Indanthrene Blue watercolor for this.

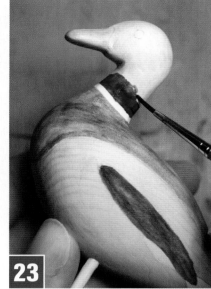

23

Paint the head. For this, I use Winsor & Newton Viridian Hue watercolor. You can make this quite a dark coat by applying several coats. Try to get a nice even finish all over.

24

Paint the eyes and bill black. For this, I use Winsor & Newton Ivory Black. You should also use this to paint a small patch at the tip of the bill.

25

Paint the legs and feet. For these, go with a bright orange. I use Winsor & Newton Transparent Orange. Try not to get any of the orange on the gray underside of the duck.

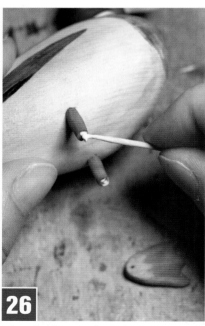

26

Glue the feet to the legs. A tiny bit of wood glue will do the trick.

TOOLS AND MATERIALS

- Saw
- Sloyd knife (I use a Morakniv 106)
- A ¼" (6mm) #8 gouge (I use a Pfeil L 8/7)
- A ¼" (6mm) #6 gouge (I use a Pfeil L 7/6)
- ¹⁄₁₆" (2mm) drill bit and drill or pin vise
- Paintbrushes
- Pen/pencil
- Wire cutters
- Non-marring pliers
- Basswood: 1" x 3" x 4⅜" (2.5 x 7.5 x 11cm)
- Basswood base: ½" x 3½" x 4¾" (1.2 x 9 x 12cm)
- Sandpaper
- Lollipop stick
- Wood glue
- Black aluminum wire (x2): ¹⁄₁₆" (2mm) thick, ⅜" (2cm) long

PAINTS

- White watercolor
  (I use Winsor & Newton Chinese White)
- Black watercolor
  (I use Winsor & Newton Ivory Black)
- Yellow watercolor (I use Winsor & Newton Cadmium Yellow Hue)
- Blue watercolor
  (I use Winsor & Newton Indanthrene Blue)
- Titanium white acrylic
  (I use Amsterdam Titanium White)

PROJECT PATTERN ON PAGE 122.

Flying Whooper Swan

Did you know the whooper swan is the national bird of Finland? They even have it on some of their coins. In this guide, you'll not only learn how to make this majestic bird, but also how to make water. You can make several swans and hang them from a mobile or make one that's just lifting off from the water. The choice is yours.

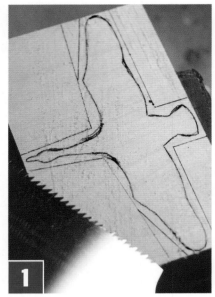

1

Copy and cut out the top view pattern. Make sure with the grain is running from the swan's beak down to its tail. Cut it out using a saw, sawing as close to the lines as possible.

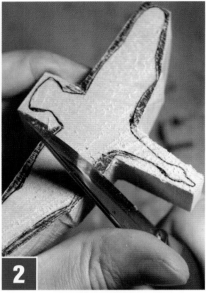

2

Remove the highlighted wood surrounding the wings. You'll be cutting across the grain, which isn't as easy as cutting along the grain. Make sure your knife is very sharp.

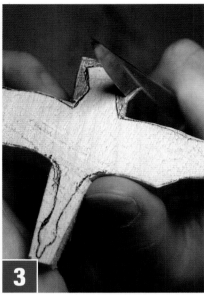

3

Remove the highlighted wood around the tail. Again, use your knife for this.

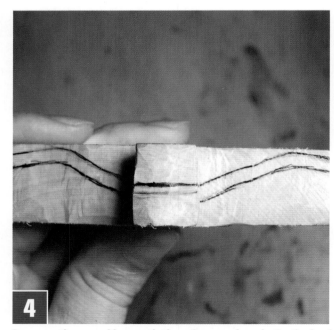

4

Remove the wood beneath the wings and neck. On the back of the tail, draw a horizontal line across the middle. Do the same on the neck. Next, copy the front view pattern onto the bird. The upper line of the wings should be at the same height as the line on the tail. Use a small gouge, such as a ¼" (6mm) #8 gouge, for this. Make sure you don't remove any of the wood that forms the body or tail of the swan. You can do this by holding the swan in your hand or clamping it down to your workbench.

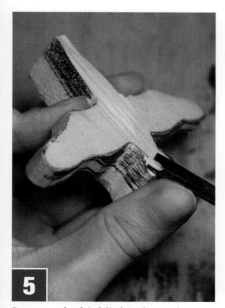

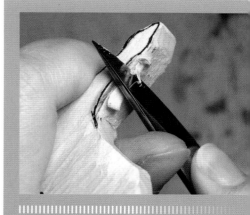

5

Remove the highlighted wood above the wings, body, and neck. Use the same small gouge as you did in the previous step. Don't put too much pressure on the wings; they'll become more and more fragile the more wood you remove. For the wingtips, switch to your knife.

6

Carve the neck and beak. Redraw the pattern of the neck on top of the bird. Remove the highlighted wood on both sides of the neck. Make sure you don't carve the beak too narrow. It's better to leave a little extra wood now and remove it later.

TIP: To prevent accidentally cutting off the sides of the head, carve against the grain just behind the head. This stop cut doesn't have to be across the entire length of the neck. It's just there to stop your cut when you're carving from the body toward the head.

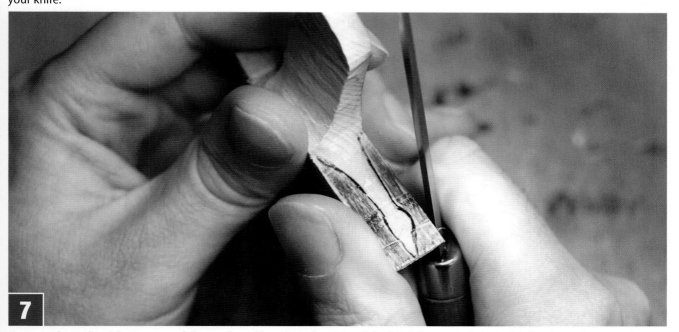

7

Copy or draw the side pattern of the neck and head on the side of the bird. Remove all the highlighted wood surrounding the neck and head.

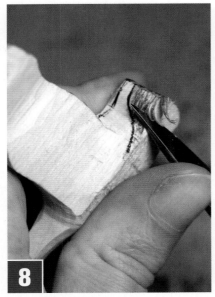

8

Carve the tail. Draw a tail on the back of the bird. Start roughly under the end of the wings and carve upward toward the end of the tail.

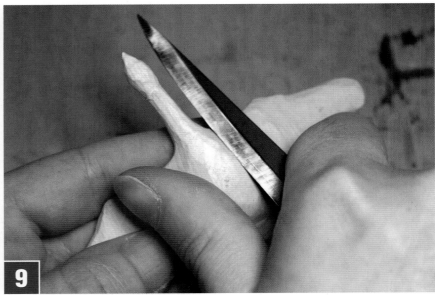

9

Start rounding off the entire bird. When rounding off the wings, remember the direction of the grain. Ideally, you're carving from the middle of the wing outward. This way, you're cutting along the grain and getting the smoothest finish. I find this easiest to do by starting the cut with the base of my knife, cutting sideways and pulling back on the knife, ending the cut when I reach the tip of my knife. Remember to not use too much pressure on the delicate wings. On the underside of the bird, make the body taper to the neck. This will elongate the neck.

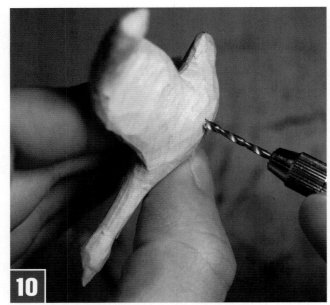

10

Drill two holes for the legs. Use a ¹⁄₁₆" (2mm) drill bit. Drill the holes roughly 2" (5.1cm) from the tip of the beak. This should place them about two thirds of the way back of the wings and ³⁄₁₆" (5mm) from the middle. Use an awl to make a starting point for the drill bit to prevent it from slipping. Now drill two holes, ⁹⁄₃₂"–⁵⁄₁₆" (7–8mm) deep. Draw a couple of lines on your drill bit; this will help you get the same depth on both sides.

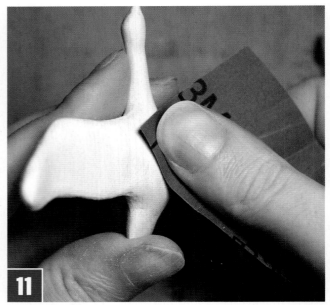

11

Begin sanding. Start sanding the bird with 80-grit sandpaper. Don't sand the head or beak with this coarse paper; it is too rough and will take away too much wood. Then move on to 150-grit sandpaper and sand the entire bird again. Paying special attention to the head and beak. Make sure the beak doesn't become too pointy in the sanding process. Then move on to 320, and finally, 600 grit.

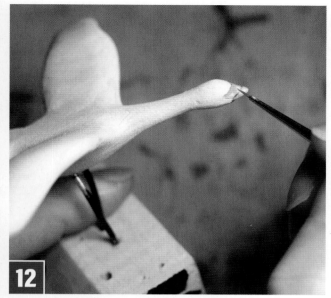

Paint the lighter parts. Copy the design of the head and beak onto the bird and start painting. Begin with the lightest part: the entirely white body. Use a paint like Winsor & Newton Chinese White watercolor for this. You might have to apply more than one coat to entirely cover the wood and get a nice finish.

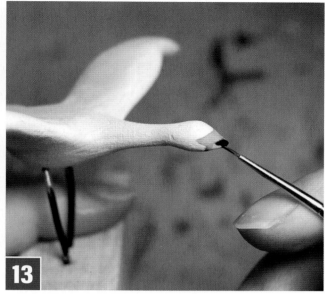

Paint the beak. Let the paint completely dry before moving on to the yellow parts on the face. Use a warm yellow color for this, (I use Winsor & Newton Cadmium Yellow Hue watercolor). Then, paint the tip of the beak with a black paint (I use Winsor & Newton Ivory Black watercolor).

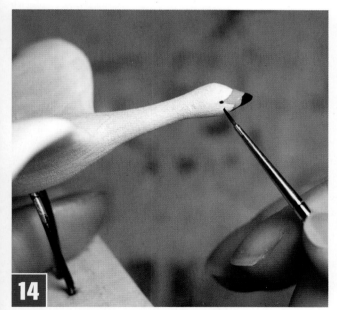

Add a tiny black eye just behind the yellow part of the face. This tiny black dot has a massive impact on the overall look of the bird.

Carve the base. On the base, draw several diagonal lines. They shouldn't be perfectly straight, draw them a bit wavy. With a slightly curved gouge, such as a ¼" (6mm) #6 gouge, remove the wood along the direction of the lines you drew. Make long and short cuts, shallow and deeper cuts. Don't make it too neat. The deeper you cut, the rougher the water will look in the final result.

16

Sand the base. Give it a light sanding with 320-grit sandpaper. This is just to get rid of any pencil marks that are left and any potential splinters.

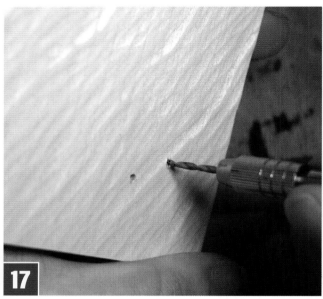

17

Drill two holes in the base for the swan's legs. Use a ³⁄₁₆" (5mm) bit. Don't drill the holes right next to each other. Doing this will place one leg in front of the other one, creating the illusion that the swan is running on the water and getting ready to take off.

18

Paint the base with blue. Using a large brush, paint the base with a blue color, like Winsor & Newton Indanthrene Blue. Make some parts darker and leave some lighter for a more natural effect.

19

Paint the waves. With a flat brush, drybrush some white acrylic paint on the "waves." This will highlight them, adding more depth to the base. Don't get too much paint on your brush; you don't want a thick layer of paint on the waves.

20

Paint the sides of the base white. You might have to sand the sides first to remove any blue paint and give it a nice finish.

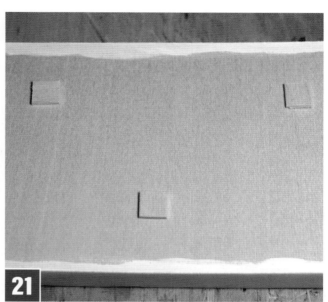

21

Glue three small pieces of a craft stick to the underside of the base. This will lift the entire base off the ground, giving it a nicer look.

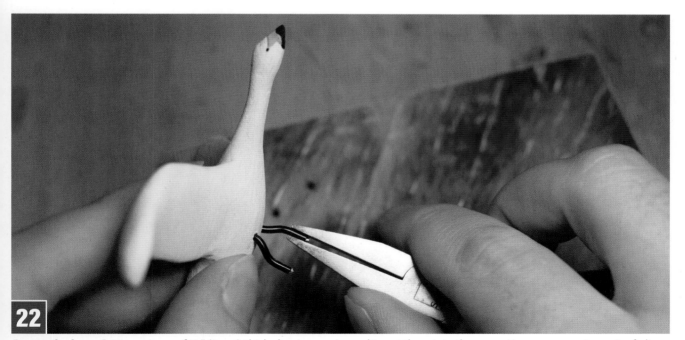

22

Create the legs. Cut two pieces of ¹⁄₁₆" (2mm)-thick aluminum wire and insert them into the swan. Use a non-marring pair of pliers to bend them so they will fit into the holes on the base.

Emperor Penguin

One of the most recognizable birds in the world: the emperor penguin. It's a stunning bird to make, but without paint, it sort of resembles a cocktail shaker. The emperor penguin is the biggest penguin, and the contrast between the white belly and the black wings and back makes it a gorgeous piece.

TOOLS AND MATERIALS

- Saw
- Sloyd knife (I use a Morakniv 106)
- Detailing knife (I use a Flexcut KN13)
- Pen/pencil
- Paintbrushes
- A ⁵⁄₁₆" (8mm) #5 gouge (I use a Pfeil L 5/8)
- A ¹⁄₃₂" (1mm) #11 gouge (I use a Pfeil L 11/1)
- A ⅛" (3mm) #11 gouge (I use a Pfeil L 11/3)
- Basswood: 2" x 2⅜" x 5" (5 x 6 x 12.6cm)
- Sandpaper: 80, 150, 320 and 600 grit
- Chestnut wood wax
- Paper towels
- Cloth

PAINTS

- Yellow watercolor (I use Winsor & Newton Cadmium Yellow Deep)
- Black watercolor (I use Winsor & Newton Ivory Black)
- White watercolor (I use Winsor & Newton Chinese White)

PROJECT PATTERN ON PAGE 124.

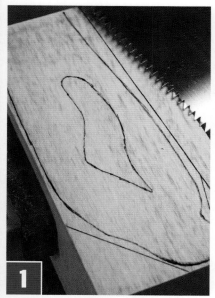

1

Copy and cut out the side view pattern. Copy the pattern onto your block of wood with the grain running from the top of the penguin's head down to its feet. Use a saw to cut it out, sawing as close to the lines as possible.

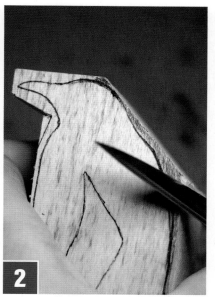

2

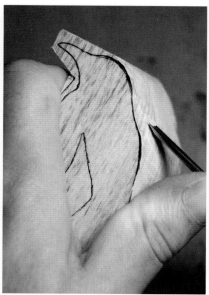

Remove the highlighted wood down the back of the penguin. Work your way up to roughly the top of the head. As a handy guide, draw a couple of lines on the bottom, lining up with the pattern. This way you'll have a target to carve to. If you have trouble removing the wood behind the head, you can use a small gouge. A fairly flat/curved one, like a 5/16" (8mm) #5 gouge, will work perfectly. Make sure you get a clean finish.

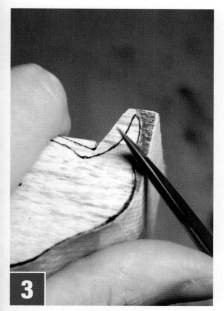

3

Remove the highlighted wood above the beak. For this, you can use either your knife or a small gouge, such as the 5/16" (8mm) #5 gouge you used in the previous step.

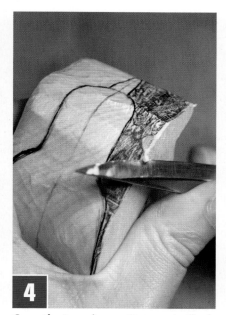

4

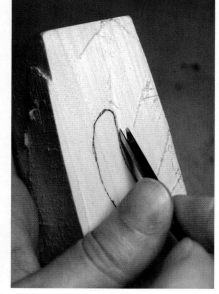

Copy the top view pattern onto the back of the penguin and the design of the wing on the right side. You can use the two lines on the bottom to line up the pattern, so you get the wing in the same place as the one on the left. Remove all the highlighted wood on the right side. Make sure you don't cut away the wing! Use a small gouge, such as a 1/8" (3mm) #11, to carve along the outline of the wing. Use the pattern on the back to see how deep you need to carve. It'll be a shallow cut at the top of the wing, gradually getting deeper toward the end of the wing.

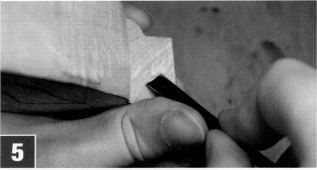

5

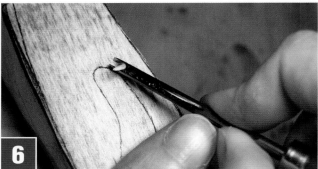

6

Remove the highlighted wood down the front of the bird.
Use a combination of your knife and a gouge to do this. I've
used the same gouge as earlier, the 5/16" (8mm) #5 gouge.

Remove the highlighted wood on the left side. For this,
you can use either your knife or a small gouge, such as the
5/16" (8mm) #5 gouge you used in the previous step.

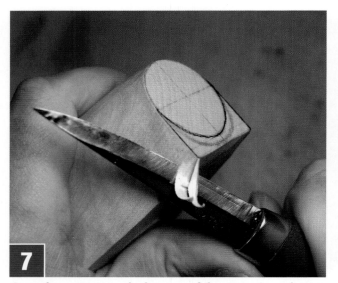

7

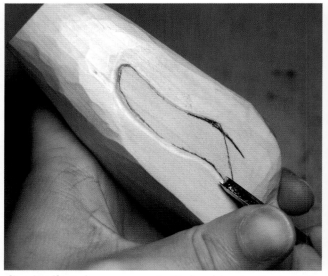

Copy the pattern on the bottom of the penguin and start rounding it off. Work your way up to the head, leaving the beak for
the next step. On the sides, make sure to keep the definition of the wings. Use a small gouge, such as a 1/8" (3mm) #11, to remove
more wood around it.

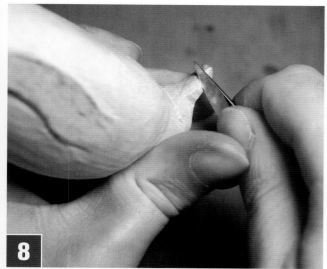

8

Carefully start rounding off the beak. When working on the underside, use only the tip of your knife. Using a wider part of your knife will result in putting too much pressure on the beak and you might break it. Due to the direction of the grain, the beak is the weakest part of the penguin. On the top part of the beak, carve from the head toward the tip. On the underside, carve from the tip toward the head. You can do some final detailing of the beak in the sanding process; that way, you'll put much less pressure on it.

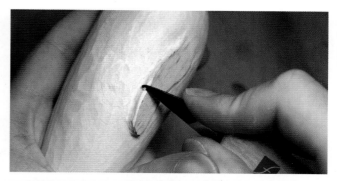

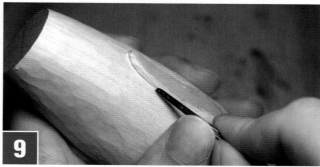

9

With the tip of your knife, round off the edges of the wings. You can use your normal knife for this or a detailing knife with a shorter blade (such as a Flexcut KN13). Then, with a very small gouge, such as a ¹⁄₃₂" (1mm) #11 gouge, carve away a thin line in the corner between the wing and the body. This will both tidy up the edges of the wing and create the illusion that the wing is separated from the body. It's best to carve more at the bottom of the wing than the top.

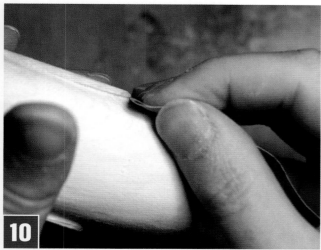

10

Begin sanding. Start sanding the penguin with 80-grit sandpaper, leaving the beak and the edges of the wings for the next stage. Then, sand with 150 grit. You can sand the beak and edges of the wings with this. When you've sanded the entire bird with 150 grit, move on to 320 grit. When sanding the beak, try to sand in only one direction, from the head toward the tip. From 320 grit, move on to the final stage with 600-grit sandpaper. Don't forget to also sand the bottom of the bird. You want to make sure it sits nice and flat on the ground.

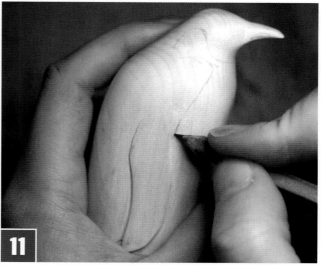

11

Draw on the design of the penguin's plumage. Using a freshly sharpened pencil will get you the cleanest and thinnest lines as possible. Try to get the plumage as symmetrical as you can.

Paint the beak. Using a warm yellow, like Winsor & Newton Cadmium Yellow Deep watercolor, paint the yellow patches on the beak. The yellow on the cheeks will follow later.

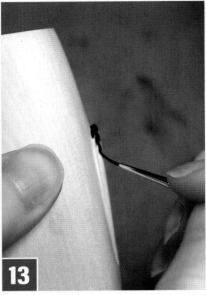

Paint the main body. For this, use a warm black. I use Winsor & Newton Ivory Black watercolor. Don't forget to also paint the edges of the wings.

Paint the white parts. I use Winsor & Newton Chinese White watercolor, but use what you like best. Paint the patches on the cheeks with this paint, too. You might need a few layers to get a good coating.

Paint the cheeks. Paint the cheeks the same yellow you used for the patches on the beak. Under the beak and the bright yellow cheek patches, paint only a thin layer of yellow. This will help it blend in with the white paint underneath. Have a paper towel or tissue at hand to blot away the paint if it is too bright.

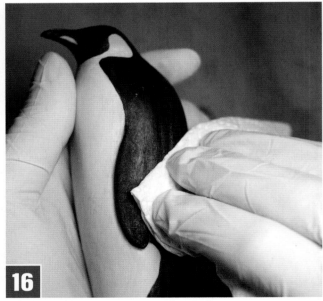

Add a wax finish. After giving the paint plenty of time to dry, apply a coat of wax. Let the wax dry for 30 seconds before buffing it to a shine by rubbing it vigorously with a cloth or paper towel.

TOOLS AND MATERIALS

- Sloyd knife (I use a Morakniv 106)
- Detail knife (I use a Flexcut KN13)
- A ³⁄₁₆" (5mm) #9 gouge (I use a Pfeil L 9/5)
- A ⅛" (3mm) #11 gouge (I use a Pfeil L 11/3)
- A ¹⁄₃₂" (1mm) #11 gouge (I use a Pfeil L 11/1)
- Pen/pencil
- ³⁄₃₂" (2.5mm) drill bit
- Pin vise, drill, or drill press
- Awl
- Needle-nose pliers
- Combination pliers
- Wire cutters
- Basswood: 1⁹⁄₁₆" x 1½" x 4⅛" (4 x 4 x 10.5cm)
- Aluminum wire: Two lengths 9" (22cm) long and 1.5mm thick
- Sandpaper: 80, 150, 320 and 600 grit

PAINTS

- Yellow watercolor
  (I use Winsor & Newton Yellow Ochre)
- White watercolor
  (I use Winsor & Newton Chinese White)
- Black watercolor
  (I use Winsor & Newton Ivory Black)
- White acrylic (I use Amsterdam Titanium White)
- Black acrylic (I use Amsterdam Oxide Black)
- Yellow acrylic (I use Van Gogh Azo Yellow Deep)

PROJECT PATTERN ON PAGE 125.

Barn Owl

This project might be one of the trickier ones in this book. Owls have a very distinctive face with lots of character in it, and you need to capture it just right. In the following steps, I'll take you along and explain how to carve and paint a barn owl.

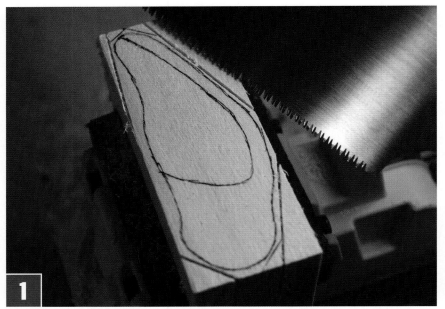

1

Copy and cut out the side view pattern. Make sure the grain runs from the shoulders down to the tail. The head, you'll notice, sits at a slight angle. Cut away as much wood as possible with the saw. You don't have to copy the face just yet, as it isn't needed in the first few steps. Keep one of the off cuts to test out the final finish later.

2

Remove all the highlighted wood down the back of the bird. When you've done this, draw a line down the center of the bird.

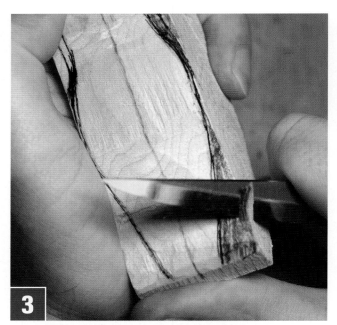

3

Copy the top view pattern on the back of the bird, and remove all the highlighted wood. This is on the right side of the bird, without the pattern on it.

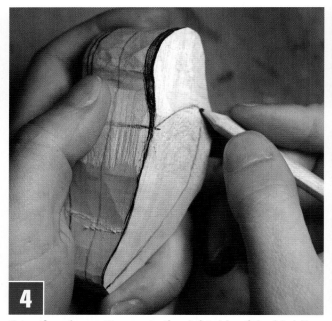

4

Copy the wing pattern onto the right side of the bird. To make this easier, draw a line across the bird where the wing starts and ends.

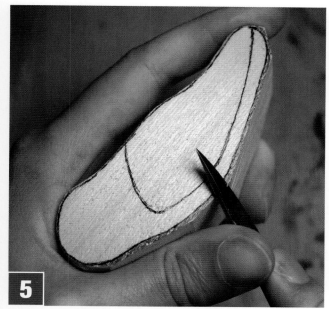

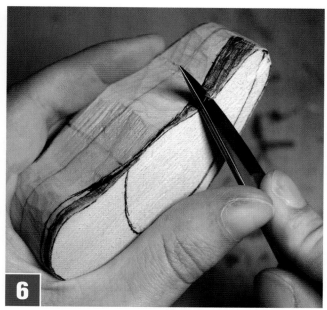

Remove all the highlighted wood down the underside of the bird. When you've done this, draw a line down the center of the entire bird.

Remove all the highlighted wood down the left side of the bird. This is the side on which you drew the pattern at the start of the project. When you've done this, redraw the pattern of the wing on this side.

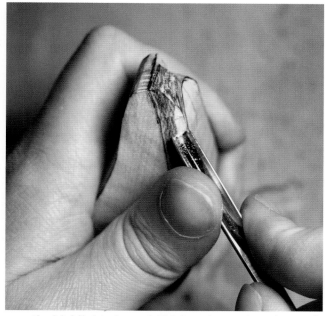

Copy the chest pattern onto the underside of the bird and remove the highlighted wood. This is easiest to do with a small gouge, such as a ³⁄₁₆" (5mm) #9 gouge. The final details are best done with a smaller and squarer gouge, such as a ⅛" (3mm) #11. Note that the tail ends roughly ³⁄₁₆" before the wings, so don't place the pattern all the way down to the tail end of the bird.

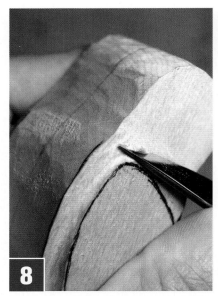

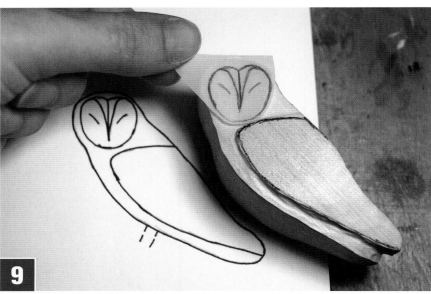

8 At the top of the wing, use your knife to create a smooth transition. Make sure the head is a completely smooth surface. Do this on both sides of the bird.

9 Copy the face onto the owl. Copy the pattern onto a small piece of tracing paper. Make sure the face is in the right orientation by comparing it to the pattern of the complete bird. It's important you use a pencil and not a pen for this step. A pen will leave traces that are difficult to sand away.

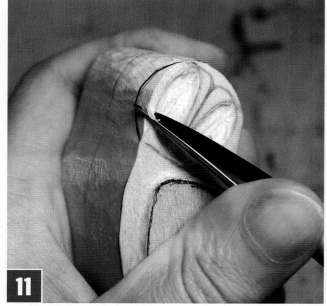

10 Begin carving the face. Using a small gouge, such as a ⅛" (3mm) #11, start carving away the wood inside the face. Use an even smaller gouge, such as a ⅓₂" (1mm) #11 gouge, for the area under the nose/beak. Carve away down to a depth of roughly ⅛". Try to get as smooth a finish as you possibly can; this will make sanding the face a lot easier.

11 Across the bottom of the face and at the eyebrows, draw a horizontal line. On the side of the face, connect the two lines with a semicircle. Cut away the wood inside this circle. Do this on both sides of the head. At the deepest part, the circle should be ³⁄₁₆" (5mm), measured from the front to the face. Make sure you don't cut away the nose/beak and eyebrows.

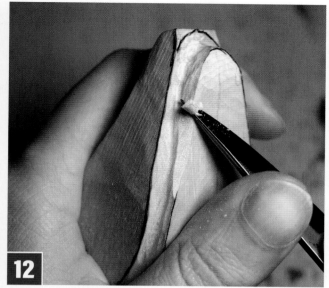

12

Draw a semicircle at the back of the wings, following the same curve as the tail. Start rounding off the body on the underside of the bird, stopping when you reach the head. You may have to need to go back with a small gouge, such as a ⅛" (3mm) #11, after having rounded of the chest/tail, cleaning up the cut that separates the wings from the body.

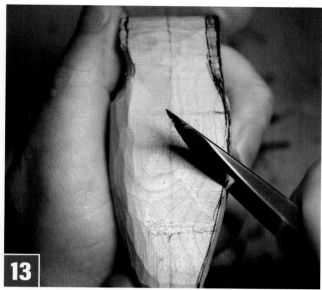

13

Round off the back of the bird. Start below the head and work your way down toward the tail.

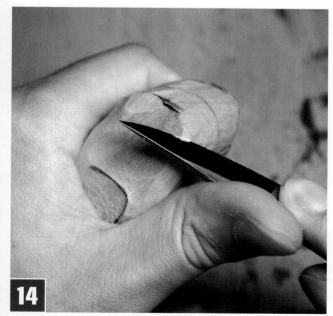

14

Round the back of the head. Owls have a fairly flat head on top, so don't carve away too much wood.

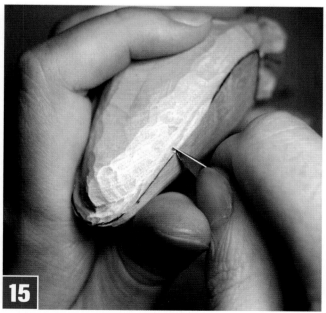

15

Round off the wings. The easiest way of doing this is by using the tip of your knife. You only have to remove the smallest amount of wood here.

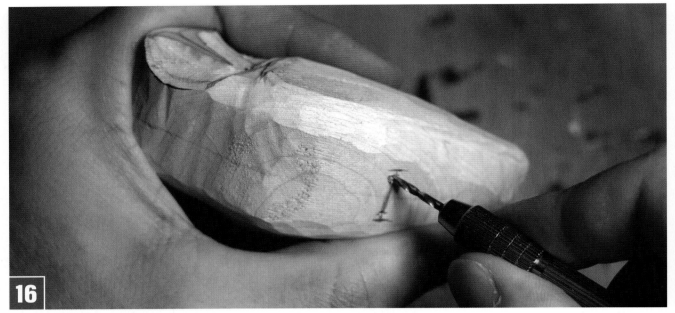

16

On the bottom, make a mark where the legs will be placed and drill the holes. Have a look at the pattern to see how far back the legs are placed. Draw a line across the center line and, on both sides, make a mark at ³⁄₁₆" (5mm) from the center line. Use an awl to make a starting point for your drill bit to sit in. Now, drill two holes with a ³⁄₃₂" (2.5mm) drill bit. I pre-drilled the holes with a ¹⁄₁₆" (2mm) bit. The holes should be ⁵⁄₈" (1.5cm) deep. To make this super easy, make a mark at ⁵⁄₈" on your drill bit with permanent marker.

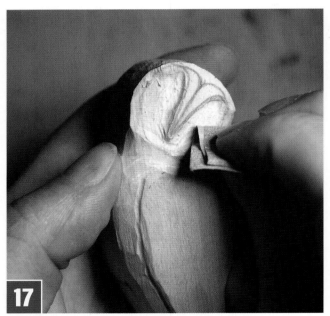

17

Begin standing the face. For this, 150 grit works best. Make sure you don't start sanding away the nose/beak and eyebrows. Get as smooth a finish as possible.

18

Draw the lines representing the eyes on the face and carve them. You can use the pattern to measure the exact location of the eyes, using the central line of the nose and measuring off that. Make sure both eyes are symmetrical and in the same location. Using a small detail knife, carefully cut away the eyes. Do this by first scoring a line down the eyes. The knife should be held at a 90-degree angle to the bird. Then, hold the knife at a 45-degree angle and make a cut underneath the line you've just scored. Make these cuts as clean as possible.

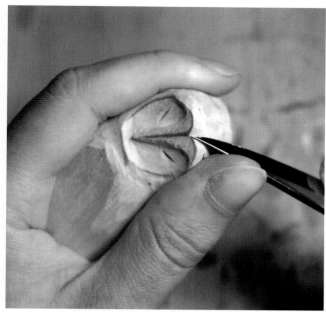

Round off the front of the head. Make sure the pattern on the face is still visible. This will help you make sure you don't carve too far. You may have to remove some wood down the chest and back to create a smooth transition between the head and body. Once satisfied, make a little indentation at the top of the head, between the two eyebrows.

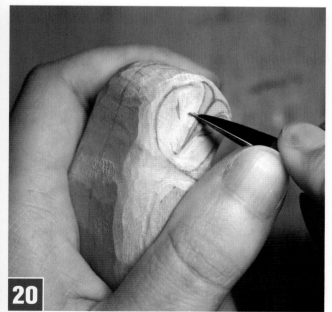
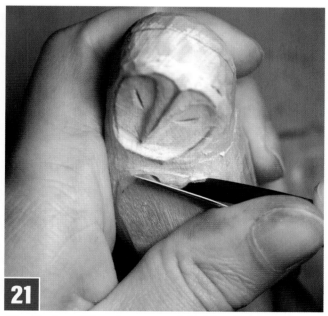

Round off the nose and eyebrows. Do this with the tip of your knife. Keep the central line intact, carving toward it from both sides. Note that because of the direction of the grain, you'll have to carve toward the top of the head on the right side of the owl's head (left side for the viewer) and down toward the tail on the other side of the nose.

Give the top of the wings more definition. Start with your knife perpendicular to the owl and rotate it while pressing down, a bit like you're revving a motorcycle.

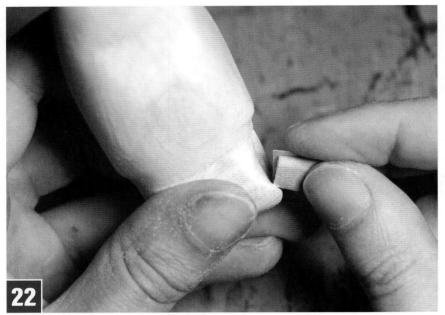

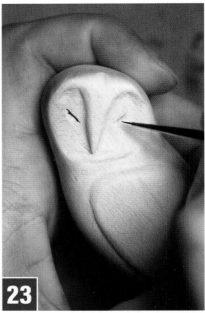

22

Sand the entire bird. Using a piece of 80 grit, start with the chest and tail and work your way around the bird until you've sanded away all the rough bits. Leave the face and edge of the wings until the next sanding, which will be done with 150 grit. When you've finished sanding with 150 grit, move to 320 grit, smoothing out the surface even more. Finish with a 600-grit sanding, wetting the bird (this will make any unsanded fibers pop up) and sanding with 600 grit one final time.

23

Paint the eyes. With a tiny brush, apply a small amount of black watercolor (I use Winsor & Newton Ivory Black) inside the eyes. Don't use too much. You can always add more after painting the rest of the face.

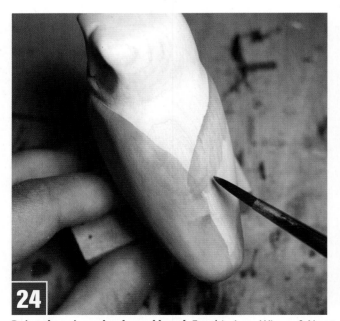

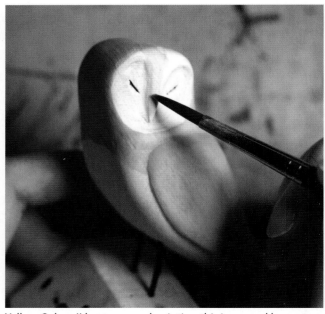

24

Paint the wings, back, and head. For this, I use Winsor & Newton Yellow Ochre. I'd recommend painting this in several layers to get the right darkness. On the back, follow an imaginary line from the wing/shoulder to the middle of the bird. Do the same on both sides and the wings will meet in the middle, creating a V shape on the back. Once done, paint the head using a thinner layer than you did with the other parts.

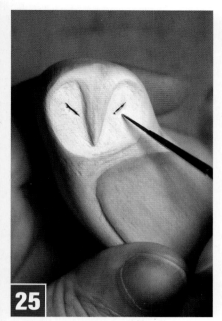

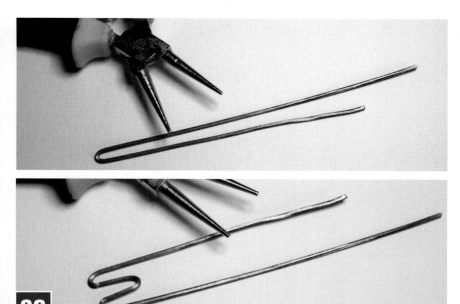

25

Paint the face and chest. These should be painted white. I used Winsor & Newton Chinese White.

26

Begin creating the legs/feet. Get a 8 ⅞" (22.5cm)-long piece of ¹⁄₁₆" (1.5mm)-thick aluminum wire and lightly sand it. Using a pair of needle-nosed pliers (the thinner, the better), make a 180-degree bend at around 4" (10cm). This first bend will end up being the middle toe. Next, make a 180-degree bend ⅜" (1cm) from your first bend. Do this on both sides, creating a sort of M shape.

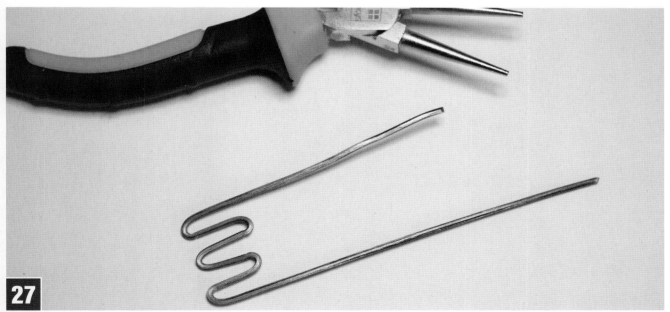

27

Make two more 180-degree bends about ⅜" (1cm) from the previous bends. You should now have three bends at the top and two at the bottom.

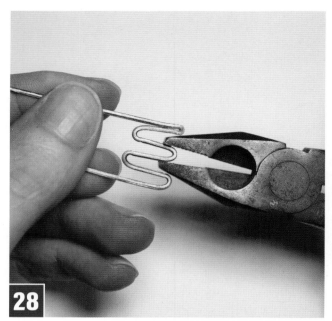

28

Squeeze the three bends at the top together with a pair of combination pliers. You now have the three front claws of the talon.

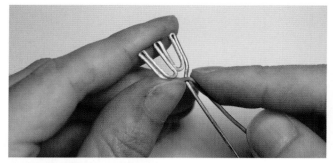

29

Bend the long end pieces. Bend them around the back of the claws until you reach the middle. Next, bend them back, essentially creating a three-pronged fork. Then, bend the shorter piece upwards, creating a 90-degree angle between it and the rest of the talon.

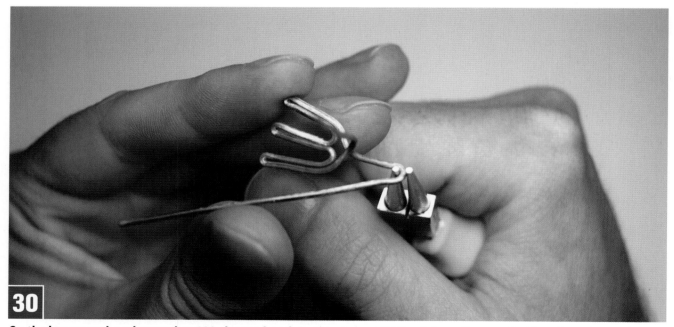

30

On the longer end, make another 180-degree bend. Do this at about ⅜" (1cm) down. Squeeze that bend together, and you now have the claw at the back of the talon.

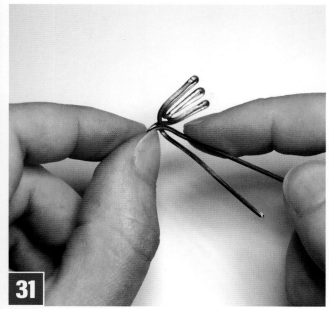

31

Bend the rest of the wire up, creating a 90-degree bend.
You now have a talon and leg.

32

With a pair of pliers, grab the two upright pieces of wire and twist them together. This is most easily done by placing the talon flat on your workbench, putting your index and middle finger on the claws, and slowly rotating the pliers.

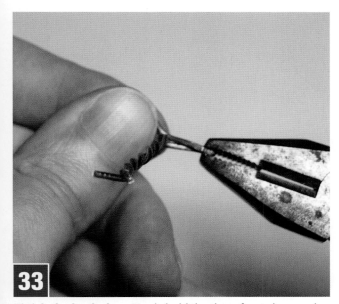

33

Finish the back claw. Firmly hold the three front claws and twist the back claw with the pliers.

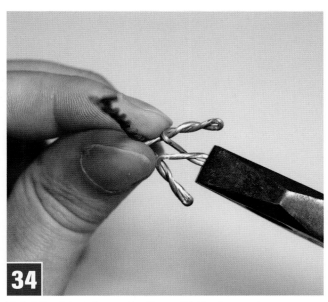

34

Twist the front claws, starting with the two outer ones.
Give all four claws the same amount of twist to make them look the same. Note that there is a hole behind the middle claw. This will be used to keep the bird securely on its perch later.

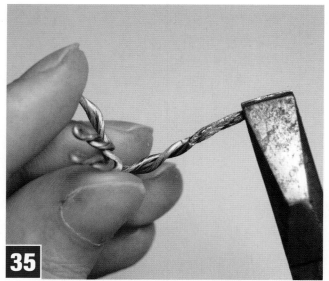

35

Cut off the extra material. Cut the leg to around 1 ³⁄₁₆" (3cm), measured from the bottom of the talon, and tightly squeeze the top half together with a pair of pliers. This will make it fit the holes you've drilled perfectly. Then, adjust the talons to fit the perch the owl will sit on. It can sit on any kind of surface. I've chosen a rustic-looking branch, but it can also sit on a flat piece of wood. If the surface you choose is uneven, you can cut a small bit off the leg to make the owl sit perfectly upright.

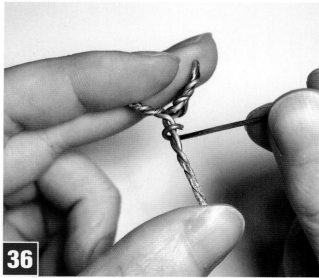

36

Make the legs thicker (optional). After adjusting the legs, you might want to make the legs look a bit thicker. To do this, you can wrap a piece of wire around it. Make a hook on one end of the wire and squeeze it tightly onto the "ankle" of the leg. Wrap the rest of the wire around the leg, using a pair of pliers at the end, to get a tight finish.

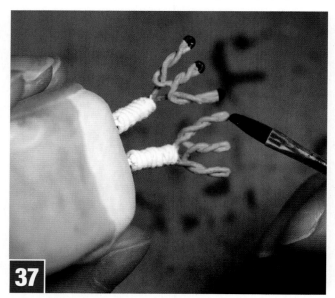

37

Paint the legs. For this, use acrylic paints. I've used a mixture of Amsterdam Titanium White and a tiny amount of Van Gogh Azo Yellow Deep. This mix should be the same color as the white chest of the bird. The talons are a dark yellow, like Van Gogh Azo Yellow Deep. The talons are a simple black. I've used Amsterdam Oxide Black. The white and yellow will need several coats to completely cover the aluminum wire.

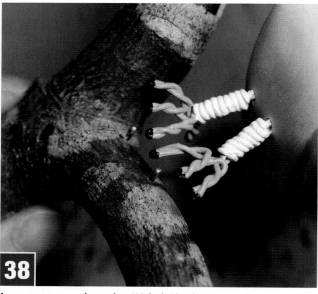

38

Insert a supporting wire. With the bird sitting on the perch, make a mark in the hole behind the middle claw. Drill a small hole, around ⅛" (2–3mm), on those marks and insert a small piece of ¹⁄₁₆" (1.5mm)-thick aluminum wire. This will keep the bird in its place. Cut these to length so they don't stick out over the talons, and paint them with a dark yellow (I've used Van Gogh Azo Yellow Deep) so you don't see them when the bird is sitting on its perch.

Charging Bull

The very first bull I ever carved was a
birthday present for my mother, as it is
the ideal present for any Taurus. It was
also one of the very first animals I have
ever made. Sometimes it is quite an
awkward carve, because of the width
of the bull, but you will end up with
a simple and elegant carving that will
make anyone happy.

TOOLS AND MATERIALS
- Saw
- Sloyd knife (I use a Morakniv 106)
- Pen
- Pencil
- A ¼" (6mm) #6 gouge (I use a Pfeil L 7/6)
- A ¼" (6mm) #8 gouge (I use a Pfeil L 8/7)
- A ³⁄₁₆" (5mm) #9 gouge (I use a Pfeil L 9/5)
- Basswood: 2⁹⁄₁₆" x 3⅛" x 5⅞" (6.5 x 8 x 15cm)
- Sandpaper
- Mineral oil
- Brush or cloth, to apply the oil

PROJECT PATTERN ON PAGE 126.

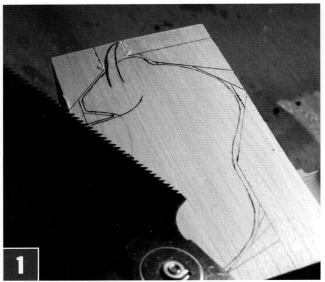

1

Copy and cut out the pattern. Make sure the grain runs from the head down to the tail. Using a saw, cut the bull out, sawing as close to the pattern as possible.

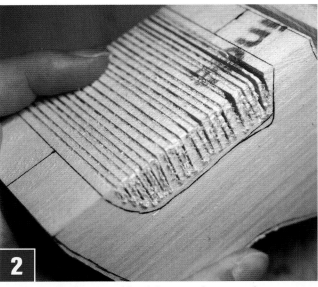

2

Between the front and back legs, make several crosscuts. Make sure you don't saw too deep. When you have cut along the entire length, it'll be easy to snap or break away the remaining wood. You can do this with your fingers, your knife, or even a flathead screwdriver.

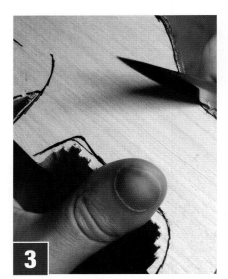

3

Remove all the highlighted wood down the back of the bull. Leave the wood around the horns intact. This will be removed at a later stage. For the area on top of the head, a small gouge such as a ¼" (6mm) #6 gouge will work much easier than trying to remove the wood with your carving knife. When all the wood has been removed, draw a line down the center of the bull.

4

Remove the wood between the legs. Draw the legs of the bull on the underside and copy the design onto the back of the back legs. The back legs are about ⅝" (1.6cm) wide, measured from the outside (this should line up with the design of the back legs) The front legs are ½" (1.2cm) wide when measured from the outside. With a small gouge, such as a ¼" (6mm) #8 gouge, remove the highlighted wood between the legs.

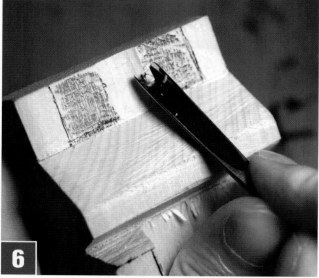

5

Remove the highlighted wood on the stomach of the bull. You can do this with your knife and the gouge you used to remove the wood between the legs. Try to get as smooth a finish as possible. This will reduce the amount of sanding you'll have to do at the end of the project.

6

Rough out the horns. Draw the horns on the front of the bull, measuring ⅜" (1cm) from the side of the head. Remove all the highlighted wood between the two horns, following the curvature of the head. I find this easiest to do with a small gouge, such as a ¼" (6mm) #8 gouge or an a ³⁄₁₆" (5mm) #9 gouge. You can cut from both sides, but make sure to draw the horns on the underside, as well.

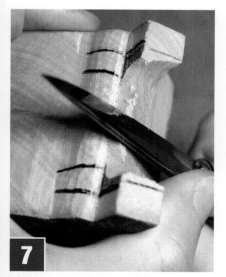

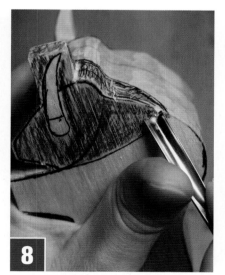

7

Clean up any gouge marks. Use your knife to do this.

8

Carve the head and neck. Copy the pattern of the head onto the head of the bull. On the right side of the bull—this is the side without the main pattern on it—copy the pattern of the horn and the line leading from the front leg up to the top of the head. Next, copy the pattern of the neck. The bottom of the neck should line up with the head and the top should line up with the lines coming up from the front legs. Start removing the highlighted wood, making sure you don't cut away any material from the horn. It is easiest to do this with a selection of small gouges, such as a ¼" (6mm) #8 gouge and a ³⁄₁₆" (5mm) #9 gouge. To prevent cutting off the tip of the horns, use your knife to cut from the tip of the horn toward the back.

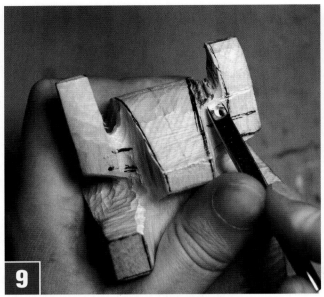

9

Remove the wood between the head and the horns.
Once you've removed most of the wood next to the head and you've gotten level to the horn, draw how the horn attaches to the head. Do this both on top and under the horn so you can carve from both ways. Then, remove the wood between the head and horn. Do this with a small gouge, such as a ³⁄₁₆" (5mm) #9 gouge, and finish up with your knife. If this is too wide, you can always use a smaller gouge.

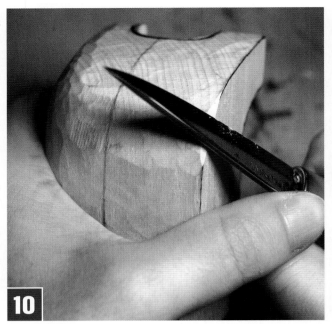

10

Round off the back, carving toward the center line. Create a smooth back, running from side to side. Carve up to the hump.

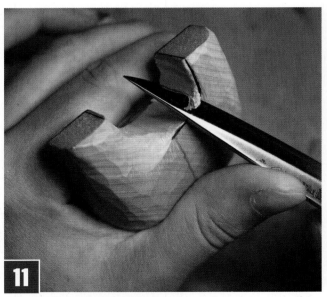

11

Round off the rest of the body. You can now also round off the area between the two back legs, the hump, and the front legs.

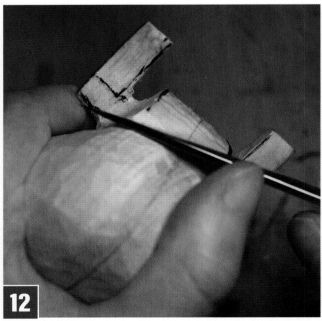

12

Thin out the hump. Just above the head, push your knife into the hump. This will allow you to make the hump narrower at the front.

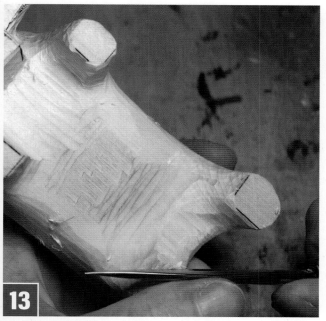

Round off the stomach and legs. Create a smooth transition from the underside to the sides. You can now also round off the insides of the legs.

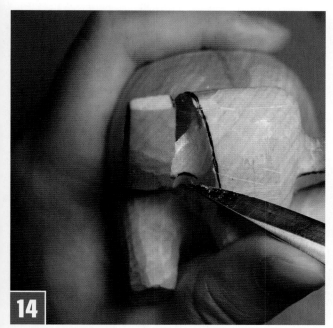

Round off the head, and transition to the legs. Keep the head quite square, even though you're rounding the hard edges. Smooth out any marks left on the side from when you worked on it with the gouge. Then, create a smooth transition between the head and legs.

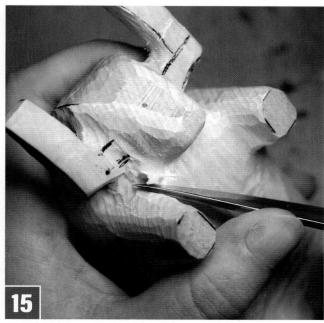

Draw a design on the horns. They can be completely straight (this is the easiest option) or follow my example and make them slightly curved.

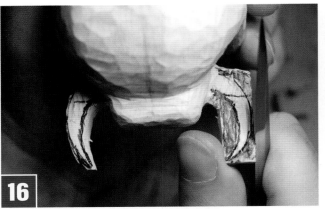 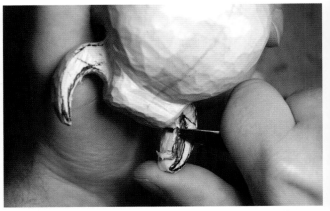

16

Refine the horns. Remove all the highlighted wood. If you went for a slightly curved horn, make sure you don't accidentally cut off the tip of the horn. The easiest way to make sure you don't do this is to make your first cuts from the tip and go toward the back.

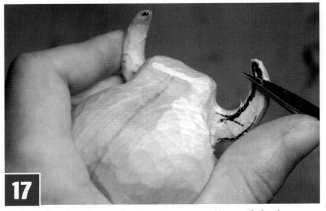 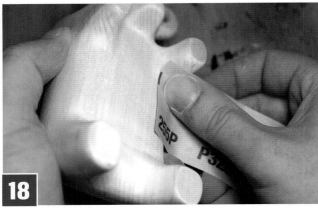

17

Using the tip of your knife, start rounding off the horns. Create a smooth transition between the horns and the head. Don't use too much pressure when making these cuts.

18

Sand the bull. Start sanding the bull with 80 grit, removing any tool marks and rough spots and rounding off any places that you couldn't reach with your knife. Continue up through 150, 320, and 600 grits until you've reached the desired smoothness.

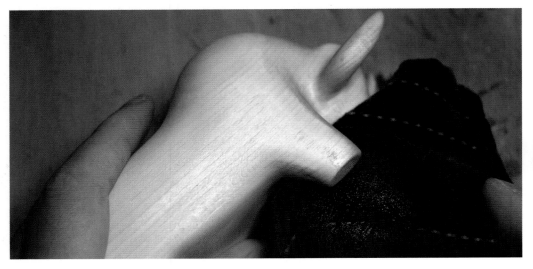

19

Apply a finish. Finish the bull with a layer of mineral oil or your oil of choice. Apply with either a brush or a cloth.

Arctic Reindeer

Several years ago, I had the pleasure of spending time with and feeding reindeer. They're very friendly and inquisitive animals. The reindeer you're about to make is based on one I've fed and petted up in Tromsø, Norway.

PROJECT PATTERN ON PAGE 127.

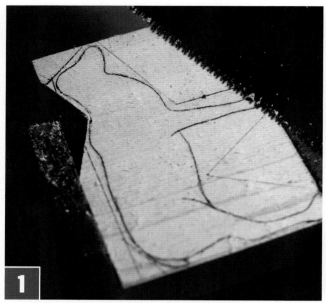

1

Copy and cut out the side view pattern. Make sure the grain runs up from the legs into the body. Use a saw to cut it out, cutting as close to the lines as possible.

2

On the bottom, mark where the feet are. This will be a handy guide when carving.

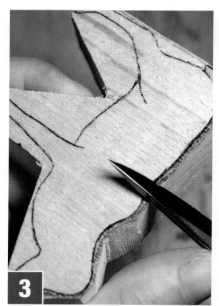

3

Remove all the highlighted wood down the back of the reindeer. When you've done this, draw a line down the center of the reindeer.

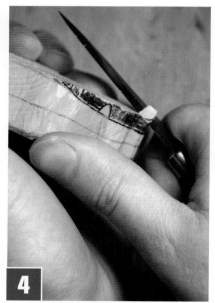

4

Copy the top view pattern onto the back of the reindeer. Remove all the highlighted wood on the left side of the reindeer. This is the side without the main pattern. Make sure you don't accidentally cut off the ear. It is easiest to keep the wood directly under the ear intact, removing it at a later stage.

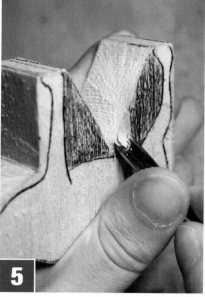

5

Remove the wood between the legs. Using a small gouge, such as a ¼" (6mm) #8 gouge, cut away the wood between the front and rear legs. Clean up the marks left by the gouge with your knife, leaving a smooth finish. Make sure you don't accidentally cut off the "toe" of the back feet.

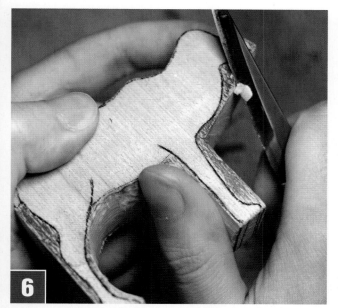

Remove all the highlighted wood behind the legs. Carve in front of the front legs and down the chest and head. Make a stop cut under the tail, to prevent you cutting it off.

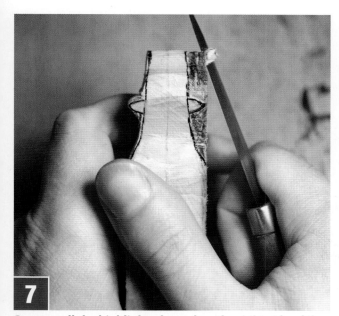

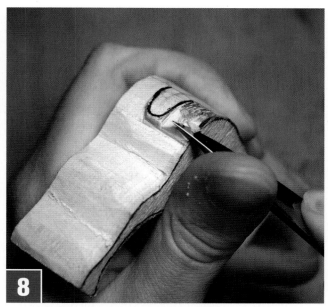

Remove all the highlighted wood on the right side of the reindeer. This is the side on which you drew the main pattern at the start of the project.

Draw the tail onto the back and begin carving. The tail is a large U-shape. Remove all the highlighted wood on either side of the tail. Create a smooth transition from the back down to the legs. When you've done this, you can round off the hard edges.

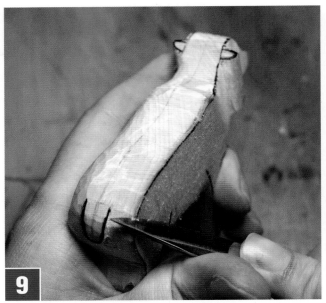

9

Round off the entire back. Go from behind the ears down to the back feet.

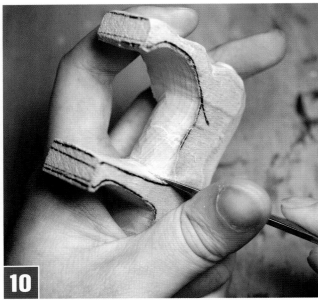

10

Round off the stomach. Push your knife in at the armpit, behind the front leg. From this point, start rounding off the stomach, carving toward the rear legs. Make sure there is a clear distinction between the legs and stomach. Do this on both sides of the reindeer. On the side without the main pattern, copy the pattern of the legs onto the reindeer. Just the top of the leg will be enough.

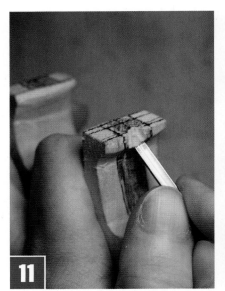

11

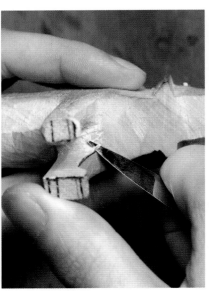

Draw on the legs or copy the pattern onto the reindeer and begin carving. The legs are ⁹⁄₃₂" (6mm) wide, measured from the outside of the block of wood. Using a small gouge, such as a ⅛" (3mm) #11, start removing the wood between the legs. Finish with a knife to create a smooth transition and round off the legs.

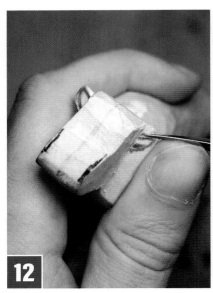

12

Draw on the ears and carve them. Do this with pencil, this will be easier to remove later on. Remove all the wood above and below the ears.

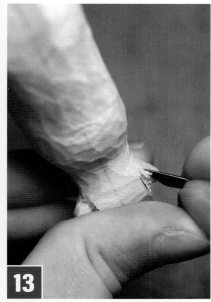

13

Round off the ears at the back. Do this carefully. Final rounding off will be done with sandpaper.

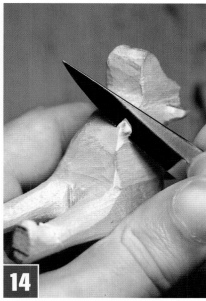

14

Round off the head and chest. Create a smooth transition between the neck and legs.

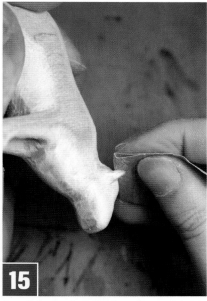

15

Sand the entire reindeer. Start with 80 grit, being gentle with the ears, so you don't sand away too much and end up with tiny ears. Then, move up through 150, 320, and 600 grits until the reindeer is smooth.

16

Create the antlers. Copy the pattern of the antlers on a small piece of walnut, making sure the grain runs from top to bottom. Drill a ¹⁄₁₆" (2mm)-deep hole in the base of the antlers. Cut the antlers out, then sand them smooth, beginning with 150 grit and moving up to 600.

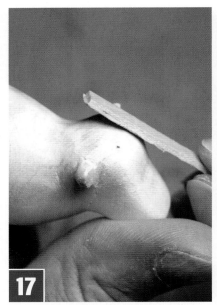
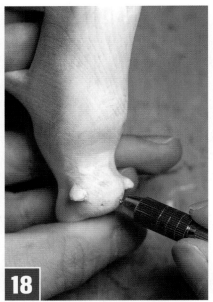
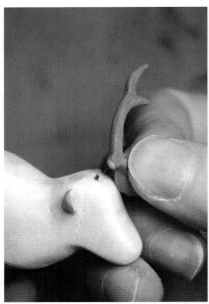

17

On top of the head, mark where the antlers will sit. On the pattern, I've marked the spot. With a small file or a piece of 150-grit sandpaper glued to a coffee stirrer or similar, create two flat areas on the head.

18

Attach the antlers. In the middle of the two flat areas, drill a ¹⁄₁₆" (2mm) deep hole. Cut two pieces of ⁵⁄₃₂" (4mm) long copper wire and insert them into the head. Put a small amount of wood glue on the bottom of the antler and place it on the head. Remove any glue that gets squeezed out and let it dry. Now that the antlers are glued to the reindeer, handle them carefully, as they are fragile. They have become more fragile like this.

19

Apply your finish of choice. I went for mineral oil and applied it with a brush. The oil will create a beautiful contrast between the dark walnut antlers and paler basswood body.

Curious Fox

After having seen my grandfather's fox, I always knew I wanted to create one of my own. The fox I have created is a lot more natural than my grandfather's and instantly recognizable as a fox. Follow along with these easy steps to carve your own stylish fox. Give it a simple finish like I did or give it its beautiful red/orange winter coat and make it a standout piece.

TOOLS AND MATERIALS

- Saw
- Sloyd knife (I use a Morakniv 106)
- A ⅛" (3mm) #11 gouge (I use a Pfeil L 11/3)
- A ¼" (6mm) #8 gouge (I use a Pfeil L 8/7)
- Detail knife (I use a Flexcut KN13)
- Basswood: 1¼" x 3¾" x 6½" (16.7 x 9.5 x 4.5cm)
- Sandpaper: 80, 150, 320, and 600 grit
- Mineral oil
- Chestnut wood wax
- Paper towel
- Rubber gloves

PROJECT PATTERN ON PAGE 128.

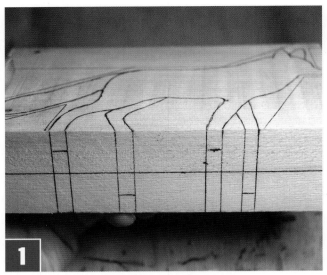
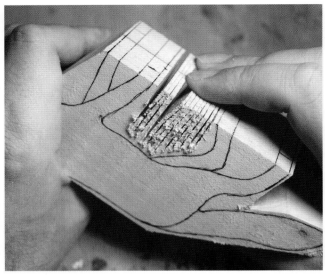

Copy and cut out the side view pattern. Copy the pattern onto both sides of your block of wood, with the grain running from the tip of the fox's nose to its tail. An easy way to make both sides line up correctly is to first draw the pattern on one side, then mark on the bottom where the legs are located. You can now use these marks to line up the pattern on the opposite side. At this stage, I also mark the width of the legs and in which side they are. For this fox, make the legs ⅜" (1cm) wide. With your saw, cut out the fox, sawing as close to the lines as possible. Between the legs, make several crosscuts with the saw. This will make it easy to break away the wood. Make sure you don't saw too deep and end up with saw marks in the stomach.

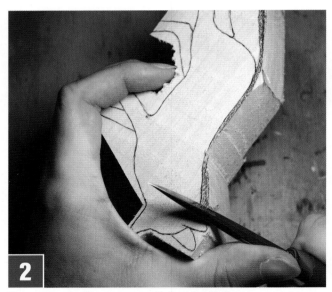
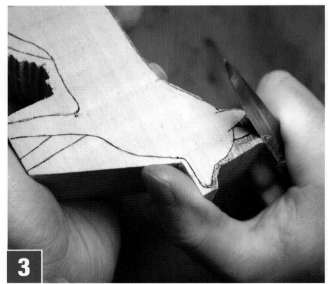

Using your knife, remove all the highlighted wood down the back of the fox. Remove it from behind the ears down to the tail.

Remove the wood in front of the ear. Go all the way down to the nose. You can use your knife for this or a small gouge, such as a ⅛" (3mm) #11.

4

Remove the highlighted wood around the legs. Use a small gouge, such as a ¼" (6mm) #8 gouge.

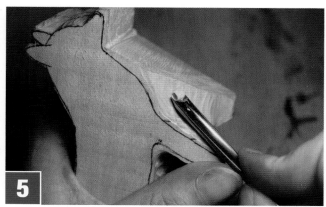

5

Remove the wood in front of the front legs up to the nose. Use the same gouge as in the previous step. Don't carve under the nose yet; this will be done at a later stage.

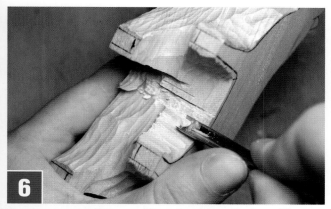

6

Continue removing wood from between the legs. When carving between the legs, draw the width on them so you know how far to carve. At the top, they curve inward, creating a U shape. At some point, you won't be able to remove any more wood with the gouge. Move on to the next step when that's the case.

7

Copy the top view pattern on the back of the fox and remove the highlighted wood on the left side. When you've removed the wood, redraw the pattern, mainly the top of the head and ears and the tail.

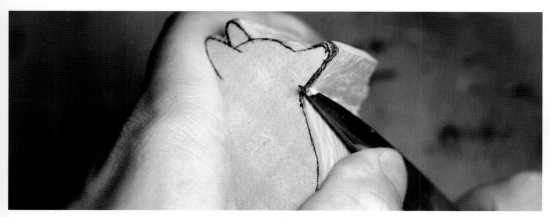

8

Remove the wood under the nose/snout. Use your knife for this.

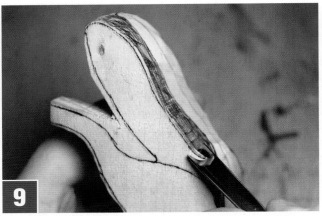
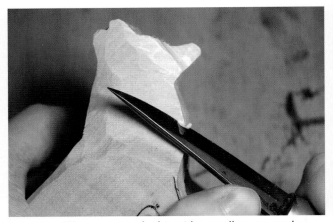

9

Remove the highlighted wood on the right side of the fox. At the tail, it will be easiest to do this with a small gouge, such as a ¼" (6mm) #8 gouge. In the front, carve upward from the top of the front legs.

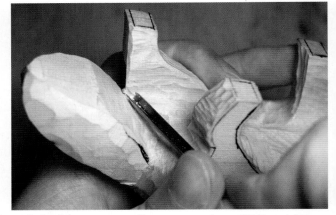

10

Further define the tail. To get in the area between the tail and the right back leg, use a smaller gouge, such as a ⅛" (3mm) #11. Redraw the pattern of the tail on the fox so you know what to carve away. You can carve from both the outside and between the legs.

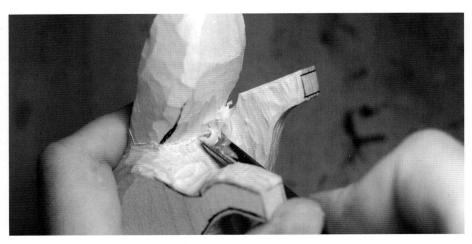

11

Carve the underside of the tail. Use your knife on the easy-to-reach places and a small gouge, such as a ¼" (6mm) #8 gouge, on the area where the tail connects to the body. Working on the tail and back leg is a case of making a few cuts on one area, which enables you to make a few other cuts in another area. You'll be turning the fox often and switching between your knife and gouges to complete this step.

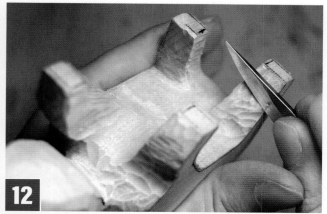

12

With your knife, carve away all the wood around the legs that you couldn't reach with the gouge. Remove all the tool marks from the gouge and on the inside of the legs and the stomach. When working with a long knife, like the Morakniv 106, make sure you don't accidentally cut into the leg opposite the one you're working on.

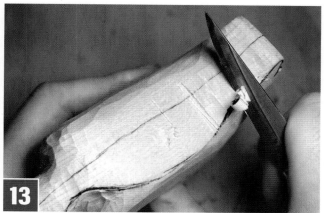

13

Start rounding off the back of the fox, from just behind the ears, down to the tail. You can draw a line down the center of the back, this will give you a target to carve to.

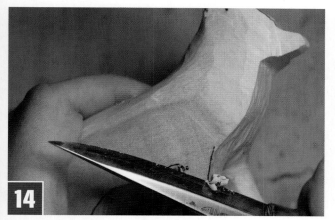

14

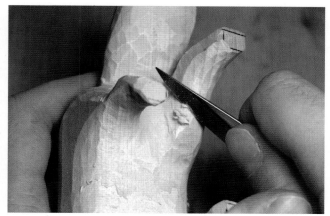

Round off the bottom half of the fox. Go from just below the head, all the way along the legs and stomach, and down to the tail. Don't forget to also round off the insides of the legs.

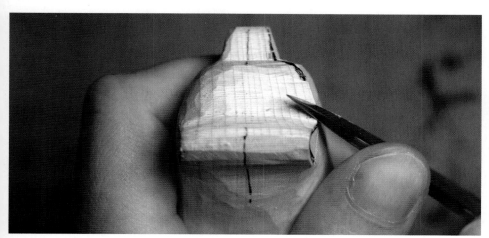

15

Round off the head and snout. Keep the snout fairly square. Leave the ears for the next step. Make sure the transition from neck to head is smooth. Take your time with this step and make small cuts.

 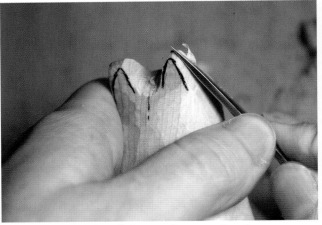

Draw a pair of triangles on the back of the head. These will become the ears. Remove all the wood surrounding them. Between the ears, use a small gouge, such as a ⅛" (3mm) #11, to carve. On the outside of the ears, it is easiest to use your knife.

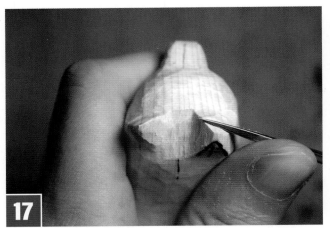 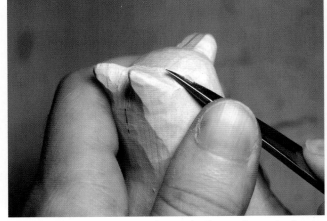

Begin angling the ears. These should either point forward or a little to the right or left. First, with your knife, cut down the front of the ear. At the front of the ears, make sure there is a smooth transition to the head.

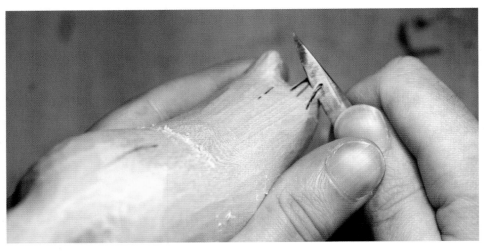

Round off the back of the ear. You can draw a line down the middle. This will give you a target to carve to.

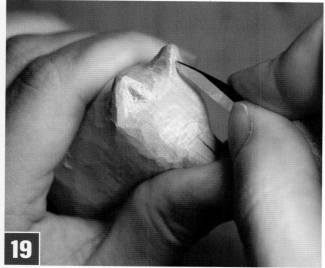

19

Begin hollowing out the ears. First make an angled cut down the front of the ear with a detailing knife. Then, make a cut on the opposite side of the ear, carving toward the first cut. You don't have to go very deep with these. Take your time and make small cuts without using too much pressure. It is possible to use your regular carving knife for this, but a knife with a shorter blade is easier to handle when working on small details.

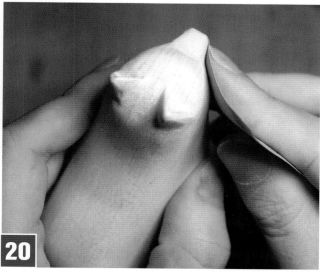

20

Begin sanding. First, sand with 80 grit. When sanding the head and nose, make sure you don't lose the shape you've carved. Then, move up to 150 grit, making sure to sand the insides of the ears and bottoms of the paws. Move on through 320 and 600 grits until you achieve a smooth finish.

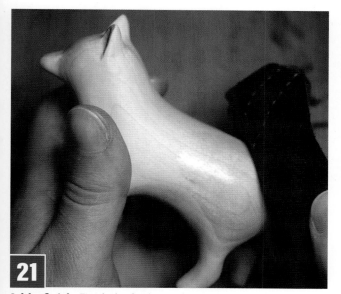

21

Add a finish. Finish the fox by applying a coat of your finish of choice. I chose mineral oil. You will most likely need a brush to apply the oil to the insides of the ears.

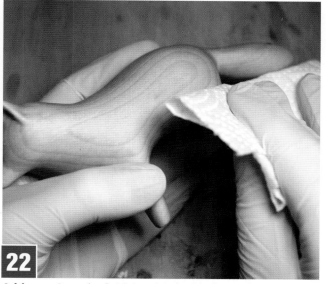

22

Add wax. Once the finish has dried, add a layer of wax. Let the wax dry for 30 seconds before buffing it to a shine with a paper towel or cloth. The final result will not be as glossy as if you'd applied the wax directly to the wood, but it will be glossier than just applying the oil.

Sitting Cat

The internet's most beloved animal, cats come in many different shapes and sizes. This is your chance to make a sitting cat and paint it the way you want. You can go for a sleek look by painting it one solid color or recreate your own cat.

TOOLS AND MATERIALS

- Sloyd knife (I use a Morakniv 106)
- Detail knife (I used a BeaverCraft C17P Universal Detail Pro)
- A 1/32" (1mm) #11 gouge (I use a Pfeil L 11/1)
- A 1/8" (3mm) #11 gouge (I use a Pfeil L 11/3)
- A 1/4" (6mm) #8 gouge (I use a Pfeil L 8/7)
- Pen/pencil
- Paintbrushes
- Burnishing tool (optional)
- Basswood: 1 1/4" x 3 3/4" x 6 1/2" (16.7 x 9.5 x 4.5cm)
- Sandpaper: 80, 150, 320, and 600 grit
- Black watercolor
  (I use Winsor & Newton Ivory Black)

PROJECT PATTERN ON PAGE 129.

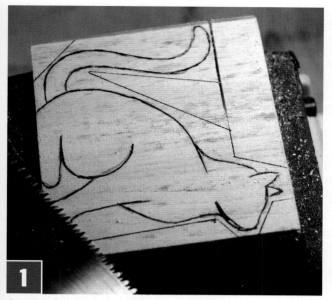 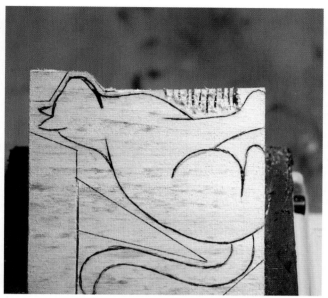

Copy and cut out the side view pattern. Make sure the grain runs from the top of the head down to the feet. Use a saw to cut it out and saw as close to the lines as possible. On the bottom, mark where the legs are located. This will be a handy guide when you start carving. Also, draw a line down the center of the cat, from the front to the back. The wood between the chest and front feet can be easily removed by making a series of small saw cuts and breaking it off. Make sure you don't saw too deep and accidentally cut into the front legs.

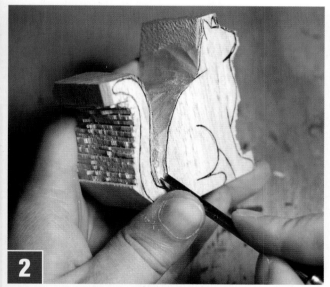 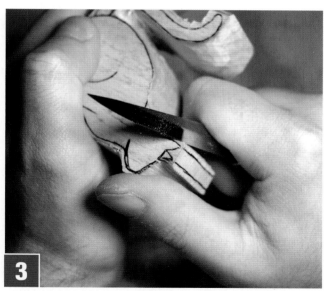

Remove all the highlighted wood. I used a BeaverCraft C17P for this step. If you can't remove all the wood between the back and the tail, that's not an issue. In a future step, the tail will be made thinner, and you'll be able to reach the middle more easily. Leaving an extra bit of wood also gives the tail some added strength, which is handy. It's easiest to remove the wood at the base of the tail with a small gouge, such as a ⅛" (3mm) #11.

Along where the ears will be, draw a line across the width of the wood. This guideline will help you see how far you can carve.

Draw the top view pattern on the back of the cat and begin carving. Draw a line down the center of the back of the cat and the tail. On the tail, measure ³⁄₁₆" (5mm) from each side of the center line. This will make the tail about ³⁄₈" (1cm) wide. Then, draw the pattern on the back of the cat. The head is about ¾" (2cm) wide. From the neck down, the body tapers down to 1 ⁹⁄₁₆" (4cm) wide at the bottom. You don't have to copy the pattern of the nose yet. Finally, remove all the highlighted wood. If you saw carefully, you can cut away a large section of the tail with the saw. Make sure you don't go too far and leave saw-marks on the back of the cat. Don't apply too much pressure, as it might cause the tail to break.

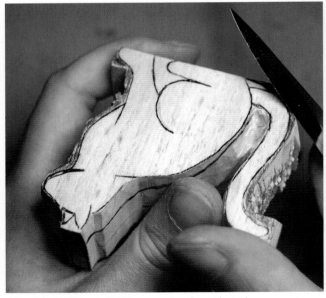

Remove all the highlighted wood down the front of the cat and at the back of the tail. When you've done that, draw a center line down the front of the cat and back of the tail.

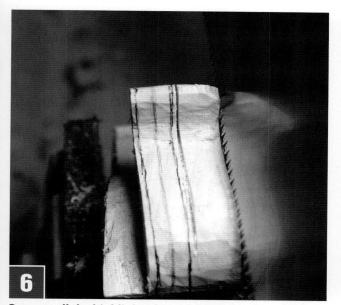

6 **Remove all the highlighted wood down the side of the cat.** This is the right side on which you drew the pattern at the start of the project. At this point, you can saw off a section of the tail, being careful not to saw too much or apply too much pressure. The more wood is removed, the more fragile the tail will become.

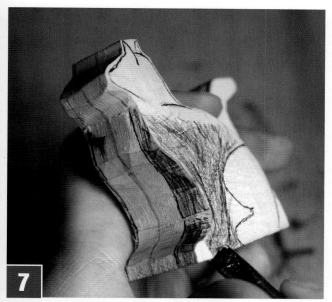

7 **Redraw the pattern on both sides of the cat.** On the front, draw two lines ⅜" (1cm) from the center line. Go from the bottom of the feet up to the head. this will create a ¾" (2cm)-wide chest and front legs.

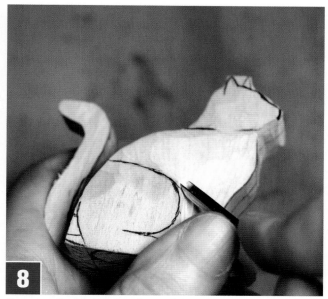

8 **Remove the highlighted wood.** Using a gouge such as a ¼" (6mm) #8 gouge, start carving. Make sure to not cut away any parts of the thighs or back feet. Use a smaller gouge, such as a ⅛" (3mm) #11, to carve around the upper parts of the thighs, creating a clear distinction between the thigh and the rest of the body.

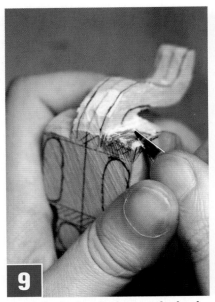

9

10

Remove the hard edges at the back.
You can now also remove the hard edges/corners at the back of the cat. This will make the entire back a smooth line from top to bottom.

Remove the highlighted wood between the legs. Use a ¼" (6mm) #8 gouge for this. Go from a shallow cut at the tail end to a deeper cut behind the front legs. At its deepest point, just behind the front legs, it should be roughly ⅝" (1.6cm) deep. Try to get as smooth a finish as possible; this will greatly reduce the amount of sanding you will have to do later. You can use a smaller gouge for the last cuts, creating that smoother finish. With a smaller gouge, such as a ⅛" (3mm) #11, you can remove the wood between the front and back legs.

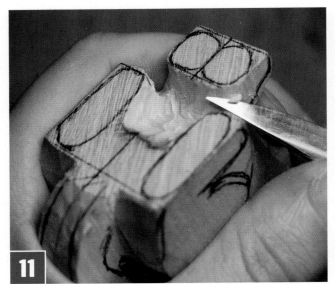

11

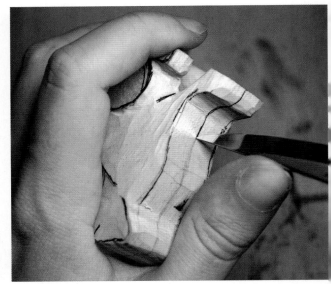

Carve a line between the two front legs, and round off the backs of the front legs. On the center line, make a line roughly 1 ⅛" (2.8cm) high. Using the very tip of your knife, make a score right down the line you've just made. Cut away the wood next to the line by making a series of diagonal cuts down it, creating a V-shaped groove. Also do this on the bottom between the two front feet. You can also do this on the back of the front legs. This place is a lot harder to reach, and it won't be visible in the final product, so it's entirely up to you if you want to do this. Round the hard edges off the backs of the front legs.

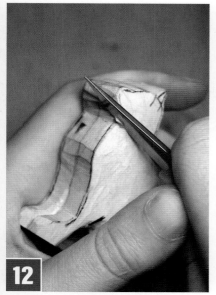

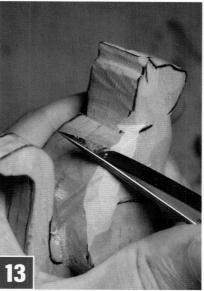

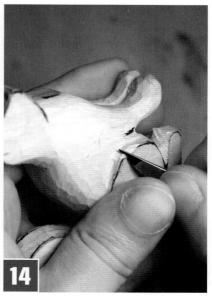

12

Round off the front legs and chest.
Under the cat's chin/cheeks, make a
stop cut by placing your knife on the
wood and pushing it right down into
the wood. This will prevent you from
accidentally removing wood from the
face you don't want to remove.

13

Start rounding off the back of the cat.
Make a small cut at the back of the head,
pushing the sides in.

14

**Using the tip of your knife, start
rounding off the thighs and back feet.**
Make a smooth transition between the
thigh and back while still maintaining a
clear distinction between the two.

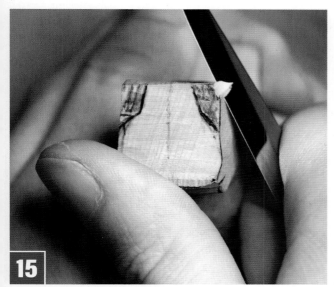

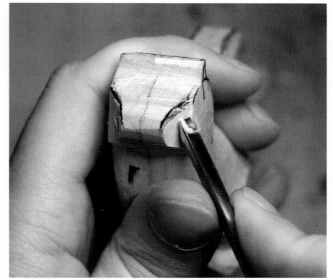

15

Copy the pattern of the nose onto the head, and remove all the highlighted wood. Remember, the direction of the grain is
running from top to bottom. I find this step is easiest to do by cutting away the wood with my knife and doing the final cuts with a small
gouge such as a ⅛" (3mm) #11. Make sure you end up with a fairly smooth surface.

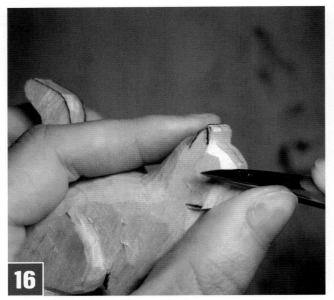
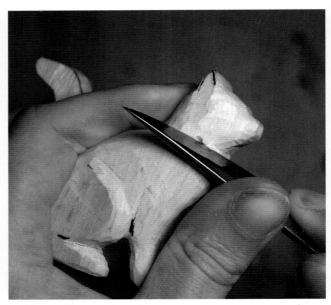

16 Round off the head. Don't touch the ears yet; this will come in the next step. You may have to carve away some more wood down the chest area, ensuring there's a smooth transition between the head and chest. The same applies for the back of the head and the back of the cat.

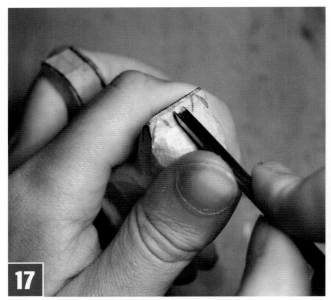

17 Draw the ears on the head and remove all the wood between them. I use a ⅛" (3mm) #11 gouge to start off with and do the last few cuts with my knife. On the outside, it's easiest to do everything with the knife.

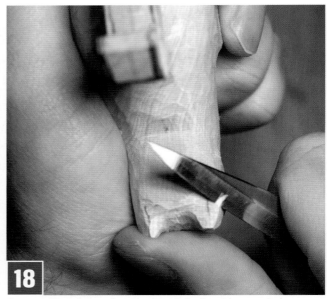

18 Draw a line down the center of the back on each ear. Using your knife, round off the ears to this line. After working on the ears, you might feel the head can be made a little bit narrower. Carve until you are happy with the look.

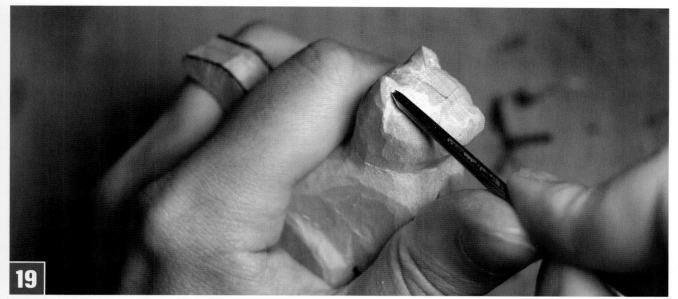

19

Hollow out the ears. For this, use a very small gouge, such as a ⅟₃₂" (1mm) #11. Do this with extreme care. It's a small area you're working on, and it's very easy to accidentally slip with your gouge and end up removing too much wood. The best way to hollow out the ears is to make the first cut going down from the tip of the ear, followed by a cut going up from the base. All this should be done using very little pressure on the tool. Try to get as clean a finish as possible. This will reduce the amount of sanding you have to do later on.

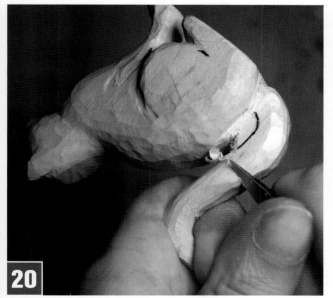

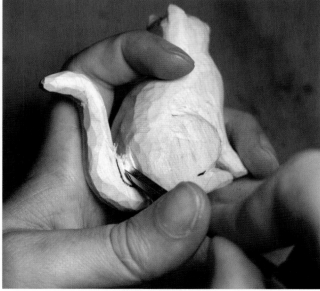

20

Redraw the pattern on the tail, if needed, and start rounding it off. Start at the tip and slowly work your way down to the base. Holding the cat by the tail is probably the best way to hold the cat. By doing so, you can't put too much pressure on the tail. If you left a bit of wood between the back and tail earlier, you can remove that now. You can do this with a small gouge, such as a ⅛" (3mm) #11 or even a ⅟₃₂" (1mm) #11 gouge.

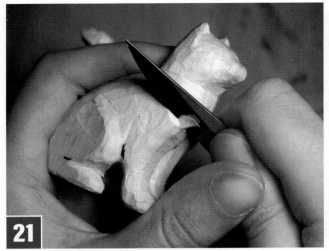

21

Adjust as needed. My cat felt a bit too wide at the front, so this is the perfect time to make some final adjustments before sanding. If you feel you can't quite get the nose/face right, draw a pair of eyes on the face. This should steer you in the right direction. No need to be precise; two small circles is more than enough.

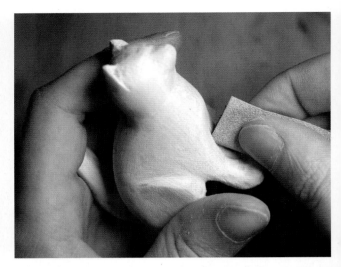

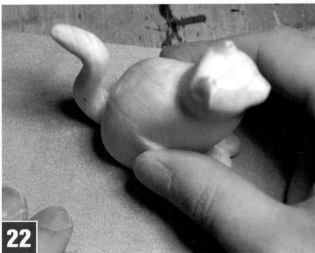

22

Begin sanding. Start sanding with 80 grit to get rid of all the bumps and ridges very quickly. Avoid the head with this coarse paper, as it will be too rough for it. When sanding between the tail and the back, you can use a thin coffee stirrer stick or similar to make sure you can get in there well. The coffee stirrer is flexible enough to prevent putting too much pressure on the tail. Between the front legs and on the insides of the ears, use a piece of folded-up, 150-grit sandpaper. After sanding the entire cat with 150 grit, move on to 320 grit and keep sanding until smooth. From there move on to 600 grit, wet it under running water, and sand again when it has completely dried. This will make any faults stand out and help you get a smooth finish.

23

Paint the cat. I've painted my cat a light gray by applying two very thin coats of Winsor & Newton Ivory Black. This will create a soft and fuzzy look. Cats come in many colors, so do what you like! If you'd like it to look a bit glossier, you can use a burnishing tool.

Walking Bear

I have seen Kodiak bears in a zoo, and they always look so friendly and cuddly, you just want to pet them. I wouldn't advise petting a real bear, but you can pet your own wooden version. This one is painted like a Kodiak, but if you leave the wood bare, you'll have a polar bear!

TOOLS AND MATERIALS
- Basswood: 2¼" x 3¾" x 6¼" (5.5 x 9.5 x 16cm)
- Sandpaper: 80, 150, 320 and 600 grit
- Chestnut wood wax
- Rubber gloves
- Tools
- Saw
- Sloyd knife (I use a Morakniv 106)
- Pen/pencil
- A ¼" (6mm) #8 gouge (I use a Pfeil L 8/7)
- Paper towel/cloth

PAINTS
- Burnt umber watercolor (I use Winsor & Newton)

PROJECT PATTERN ON PAGE 130.

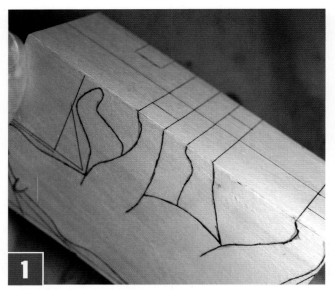

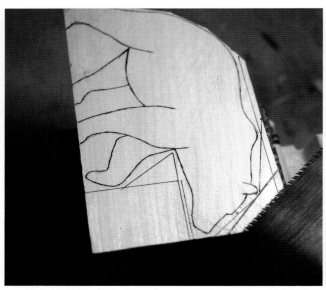

Copy and cut out the side view pattern. Make sure the grain is running from the tip of the bear's nose to the back leg. Copy the pattern on both sides of the block, making sure the legs line up. Do this by marking on the bottom where the legs are positioned. In this step, I've also drawn a line down the center and marked the width of the legs. The back legs are roughly 11/16" (1.75cm) wide and the front legs are 5/8" (1.5cm) wide. Measure from the outside for the most accurate measurements. When you have copied the pattern on both sides of the block, cut out the bear with a saw, sawing as close to the lines as possible. Keep one of the cutoffs to test the finish at the end of the entire project.

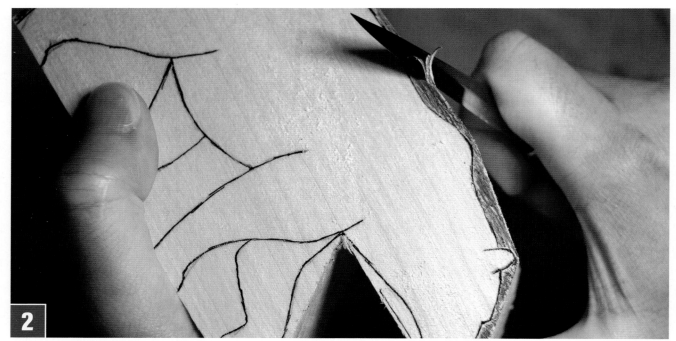

Remove all the highlighted wood down the back of the bear. Make sure you don't accidentally remove too much wood around the ears. If you can't get the face quite right, this will be easier to get right in a later step, when you've removed some wood down the side.

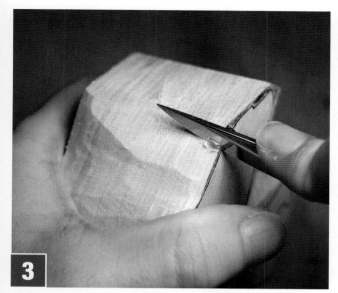

Make a stop cut behind the ears to avoid cutting into the ears or cutting them off entirely. To do this, push down your knife behind the ears. Work your way from one side of the bear to the other side.

Remove the highlighted wood around the legs. Use a small gouge, such as a ¼" (6mm) #8 gouge.

Remove the wood in front of the front legs up to the nose. Use the same gouge as in the previous step. Don't carve under the nose yet; this will be done at a later stage.

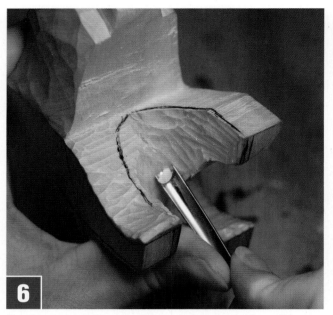

Continue removing wood from between the legs. When carving between the legs, draw the width on them so you know how far to carve. At the top, they curve inward, creating a U shape. At some point, you won't be able to remove any more wood with the gouge. Move on to the next step when that's the case. When you have removed enough wood, start refining the shape of the legs. Follow the pattern for this.

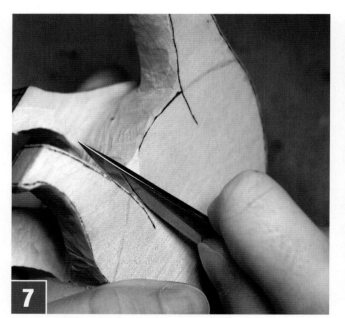

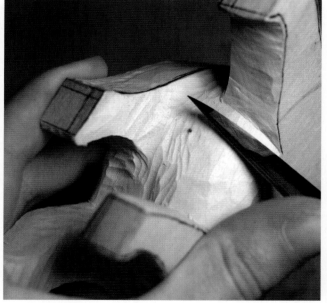

Start rounding off the stomach of the bear, between the legs. Make a small stop cut behind the front legs and in front of the back legs to make it easy to round off the stomach. Then, round off to roughly the inside of the legs.

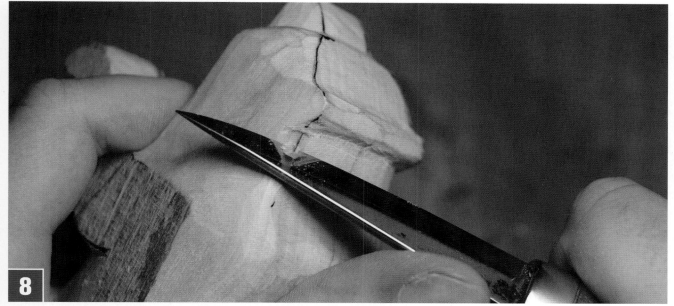

8

Start rounding off the back. Work from just behind the ears down to the back legs.

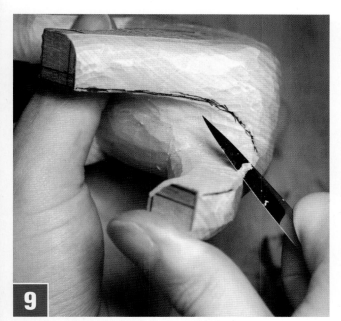

9

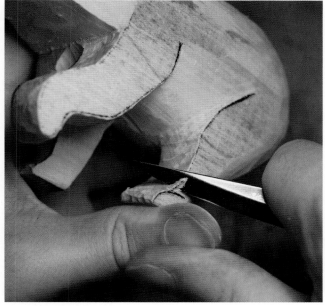

Round off the back legs. Make the ankle a bit narrower to create a clearly defined foot.

10

Round off the underside of the neck and head. Work your way from the front legs to the cheeks, not touching the snout/nose yet.

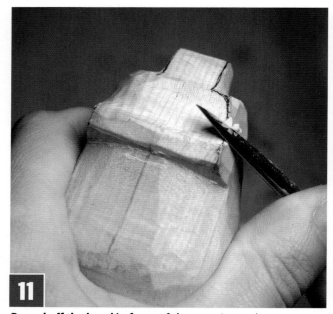

11

Round off the head in front of the ears. Leave the ears intact.

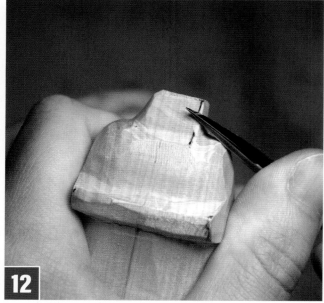

12

Round off the snout/nose. Don't make it too round; leave it fairly square. Carve a smooth transition from the cheeks to the snout/nose.

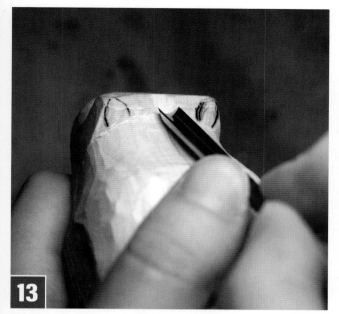

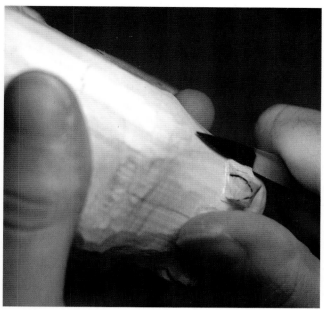

Draw a pair of ears on the bear and remove the wood surrounding them. For the middle part, I like to use a small gouge, such as the ¼" (6mm) #8 gouge used previously. On the outside, you can use your knife.

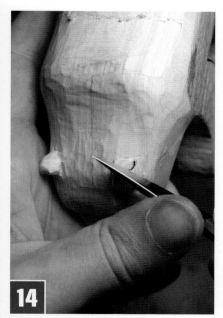

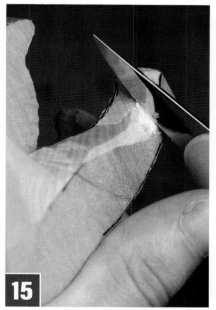

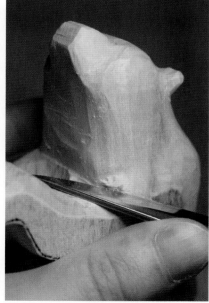

Round the ears off. Make sure there is a smooth transition going from the neck to the head, on both the top and the side.

Now round off the front legs, creating a foot on the righthand side. Make sure the transition from leg to body is smooth. You may have to remove a bit of wood down the neck to make this possible.

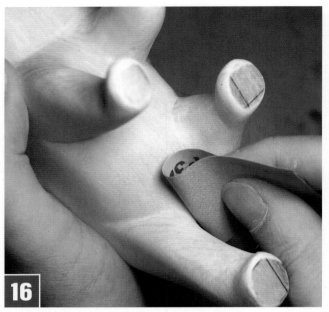

Begin sanding. Start sanding the bear with 80-grit sandpaper. Be careful around the snout, as you want to keep the square shape you've created with the knife. Once you've sanded the entire bear, move on to 150 grit. Don't forget to sand the feet. Do this on a large piece of sandpaper, putting it on a flat surface and moving the bear all over it. This will make sure the feet are level. From there, move on to 320 grit and finish with 600 grit, sanding until you've reached the desired smoothness. If you've kept one of the cutoffs to test your finish on, you can sand this at the same time.

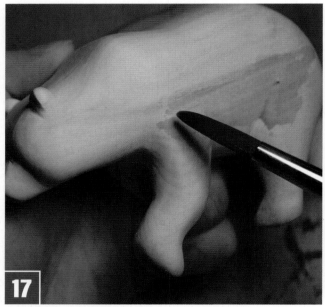

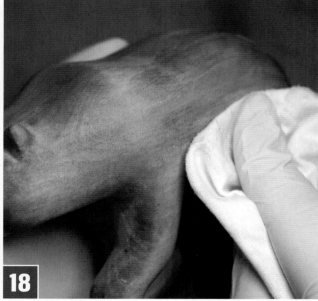

Paint the bear (optional). Using a large brush, paint the bear with a burnt umber watercolor (I use Winsor & Newton). Paint a very thin layer on so the grain will still be visible. Get your brush very wet for this. It is better to paint it too light and add another layer than paint it too dark. Let the paint dry completely before deciding whether a second layer is needed or not.

Using a clean cloth, put a layer of wax on the bear. Let it dry for 30 seconds. When the wax has dried a little bit, rub the wax out with a paper towel, polishing the bear to a shiny finish.

Howling Wolf

Almost everyone has seen or heard a howling wolf, either in the movies or maybe even in real life. In the following pages, I'll take you through the steps on how to make your very own howling wolf (actual howling not included). This is probably one of the hardest projects in the book, with many small details to get right and fiddly work in hard-to-reach places. But when you get it right, it'll be a stunning piece to carve.

TOOLS AND MATERIALS

- Saw
- Sloyd knife (I use a Morakniv 106)
- Pen/pencil
- A ¼" (6mm) #8 gouge (I use a Pfeil L 8/7)
- A ⅛" (3mm) #11 gouge (I use a Pfeil L 11/3)
- A ¹⁄₃₂" (1mm) #11 gouge (I use a Pfeil L 11/1)
- Paintbrushes
- Basswood, 1⅜" x 4⅜" x 4¼" (3.5 x 11 x 10.5cm)
- Sandpaper: 80, 150, 320, and 600 grits
- Gray watercolor (I use Winsor & Newton Payne's Gray)
- Black watercolor (I use Winsor & Newton Ivory Black)

PROJECT PATTERN ON PAGE 132.

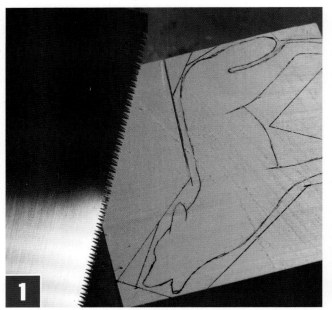 

Copy the pattern onto your block of wood, making sure the grain runs vertically, from the bottom of the feet up to the nose. Use a saw to cut it out and saw as close to the lines as possible. On the bottom of the feet, mark where they are exactly located with a few lines across the bottom. This will come in handy as a guide where to carve to.

 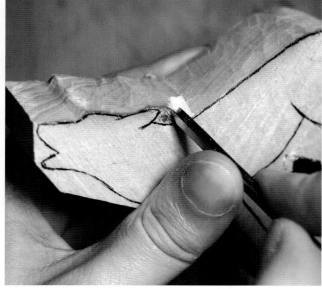

Remove all the highlighted wood down the back of the wolf. The wood between the ear and the back is easiest to remove with a small gouge, like a Pfeil L 11/3.

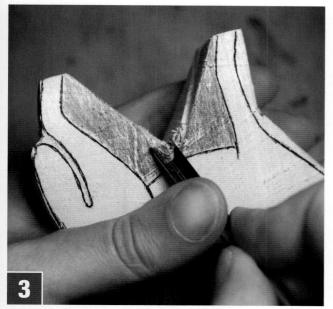

3

With a small gouge, like a Pfeil L 8/7, remove all the highlighted wood between the front and back legs. The corners where the legs meet the body can be done with a small V-shaped gouge, like a Pfeil L 11/3.

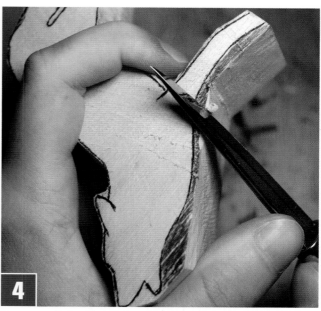

4

Remove all the highlighted wood down the front of the wolf.

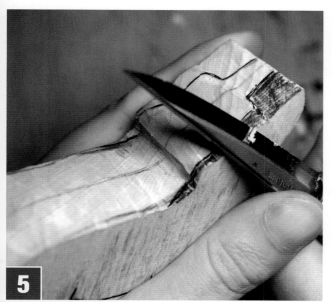

5

Copy the pattern of the head onto the wolf. Carve away the highlighted wood on the right side, this is the side without the main pattern.

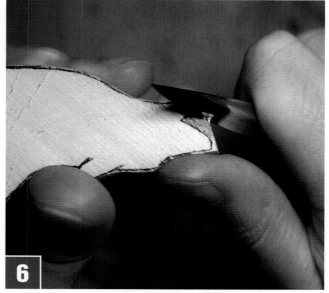

6

Carve away the highlighted wood between the upper and lower jaw. Use the tip of your knife to gently remove the wood. A nicer finish will be achieved during sanding, so don't worry if you can't remove all the wood.

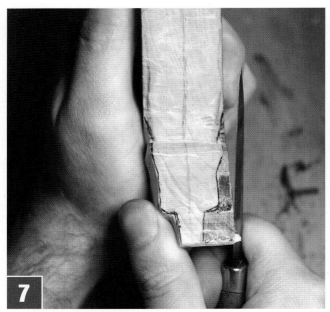

7 Remove the highlighted wood on the left side of the head. This is the side on which you drew the pattern at the start of the project. Be gentle when carving near the jaws. You don't want to accidentally chip off a piece of wood there.

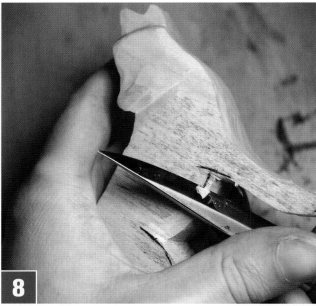

8 Copy the design of the upper legs, where the legs meet the body, onto the wolf's right side. Make a stop cut behind the front leg and round off the stomach of the wolf. Round off the stomach on both sides.

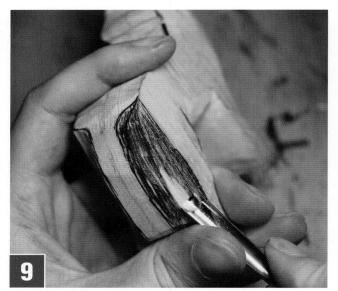

9 Copy the pattern of the tail onto the back end of the wolf. Make sure the pattern lines up with the vertical lines on the side of the wolf. Remove all the highlighted wood on both sides of the tail, making sure you don't cut away any part of the legs. This is most easily done with small gouges, such as a ¼" (6mm) #8 gouge and a ⅛" (3mm) #11, in the corner between the tail and leg. Get as clean a finish as possible and redraw the pattern of the tail on the side.

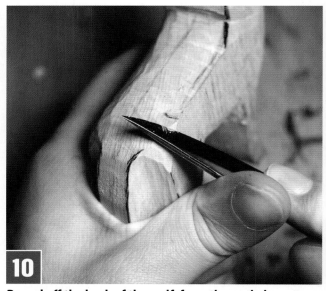

10 Round off the back of the wolf, from the neck down to the tail.

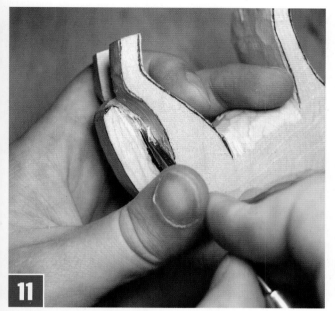
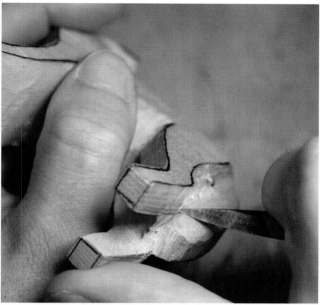

Copy the pattern of both front and rear legs onto the wolf and carve the back legs and tail. Start with slowly removing the highlighted wood between the rear legs with a small gouge, such as a ¼" (6mm) #8 gouge. You won't be able to remove all the wood from this angle. More wood will be removed when working on the tail and rounding off the legs. With a very small gouge, such as a ⅟₃₂" (1mm) #11 gouge, start removing the wood between the rear legs and tail. At the same time, you can round off the tail and legs, which will make reaching the area between the tail and legs a tad easier. This is all done in stages. First, you remove some wood between the tail and legs. This will allow you to round off the tail and legs a small bit, which in turn will let you remove some more wood between the tail and legs. Keep doing this until the entire tail has been "freed."

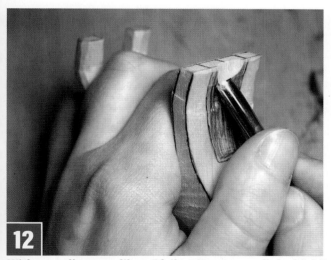
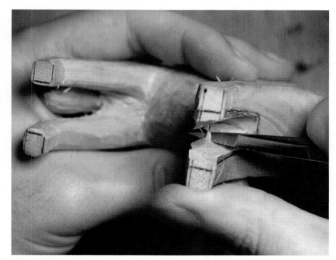

With a small gouge, like a Pfeil L 8/7, remove all the highlighted wood between the front and back legs. The corners where the legs meet the body can be done with a small V-shaped gouge, like a Pfeil L 11/3.

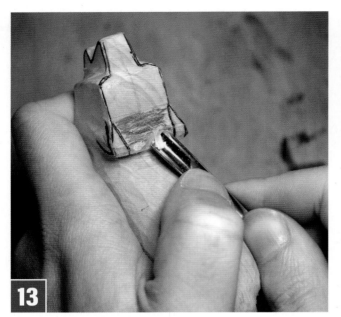

13

Remove all the highlighted wood between the ears. Create a smooth transition from the head to the neck. Because of the direction of the grain, you'll have to carve up from the neck. Also remove some excess wood under and behind the ears, which will slim down the neck a bit. Do this with your knife.

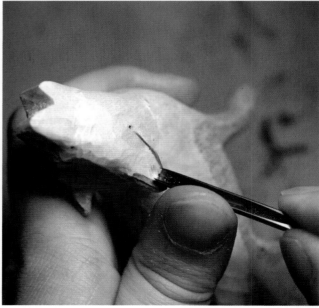

14

Start rounding off the head. Create a smooth transition between the head, neck, chest, and ears. Do not make the head too round, a fairly square head will look nicer in the end result. On the ears, draw a diagonal line from the tip of the ear down to the side where it connects to the head. Gently carve away the outside at an angle and round off the backside. Optionally, you can hollow out the ears with a small gouge, such as a ⅛" (3mm) #11. Do this by first drawing a pencil line around the outside of the ear. Then gently carve away some wood inside of this line. Don't use too much pressure when doing this, and don't try making the ear too thin.

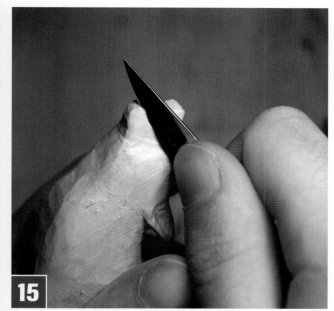

Make the bottom jaw a little bit narrower than the upper jaw. Do this gently, making small cuts and not using too much pressure.

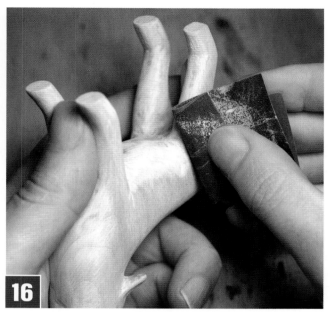

Begin sanding. Start sanding the wolf with 80-grit sandpaper, avoiding the entire muzzle/snout and inner ears. Make sure the area between the back legs and tail is completely smooth. Then move on to 150 grit, paying special attention to the muzzle/snout and inner ears. Next, move through 320 and finally 600 grit until you reach your desired smoothness.

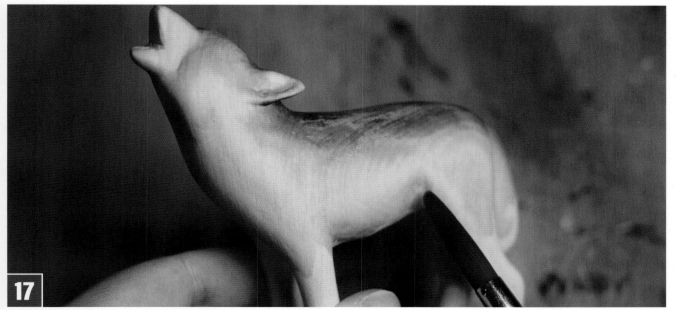

Paint the wolf. Using a fairly large brush, paint the wolf gray (I use Winsor & Newton Payne's Gray and Ivory Black). Make the wolf darker on the back. Rather than doing this in one go, add multiple layers of paint. Let the paint dry completely before applying the next layer.

Standing Bunny

I often see rabbits in the wild and they're always fun to see. Seeing one standing up, on full alert, looks even cuter. In this step-by-step guide, you'll learn how to carve your very own standing bunny.

TOOLS AND MATERIALS

- Saw
- Sloyd knife (I use a Morakniv 106)
- Detail knife (I used a BeaverCraft C17P Universal Detail Pro)
- A ⅝" (16mm) #5 gouge (I use a Pfeil L 5/16)
- A ¼" (6mm) #8 gouge (I use a Pfeil L 8/7)
- A ⅛" (3mm) #11 gouge (I use a Pfeil L 11/3)
- A ½2" (1mm) #11 gouge (I use a Pfeil L 11/1)
- A ¼" (6mm) #6 gouge (I use a Pfeil L 7/6)
- Pen/pencil
- Basswood, 2" x 2¾" x 5¼" (5 x 7 x 13.5cm)
- Sandpaper. 80, 150, 320 and 600 grit
- Mineral oil

PROJECT PATTERN ON PAGE 121.

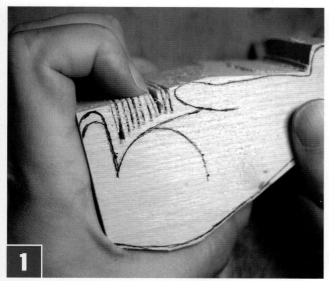

1

Copy and cut out the side view pattern. Make sure the grain is running from the tips of the ears down to the feet. Use a saw to cut it out, getting as close to the lines as possible. Between the front and back feet, make several crosscuts (making sure not to cut too far down). This will make removing the wood very easy.

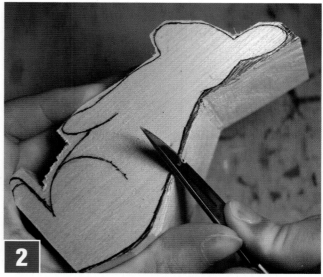

2

Using your knife, remove all the highlighted wood down the back of the rabbit. When you've done this, draw a center line down the back of the rabbit.

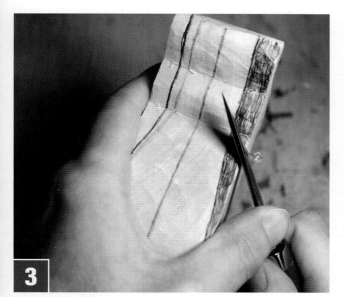

3

Copy the top view pattern onto the back of the rabbit. Then, remove all the highlighted wood down the right side of the rabbit. This is the side without the pattern on it. You can use a big gouge, such as a ⅝" (16mm) #5 gouge, to remove most of the wood. You can remove the final bits of wood with a knife.

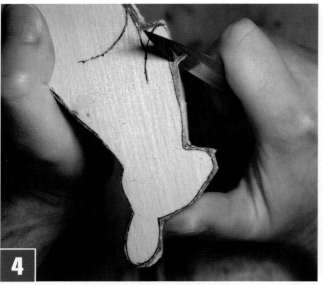
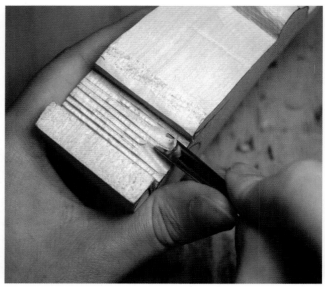

Remove all the highlighted wood down the front of the rabbit. Between the front and back legs, removing the wood is easiest done with a small gouge, such as a ¼" (6mm) #8 gouge or ⅛" (3mm) #11 gouge. Don't try yet to remove the wood between the front legs and main body; this will be done at a later stage when it is much easier to reach and there is less wood to remove. Once the wood is removed, draw a line down the middle of the rabbit, just like you've done on the back of the rabbit.

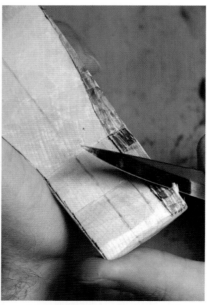
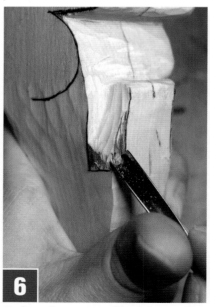

Remove all the highlighted wood down the rabbit's left side. This is the side on which you drew the pattern at the start of the project. You can again remove most of the wood with a big gouge, such as a ⅝" (16mm) #5 gouge.

Redraw the pattern of both front and back legs on both sides of the rabbit. Then, copy the provided pattern onto the front of the front legs and begin carving. Remove the wood next to the front leg with a small gouge, such as a ¼" (6mm) #8. For the smaller work, in the corner between the leg and main body, use a smaller V-shaped gouge, such as a ⅛" (3mm) #11.

7

Start rounding off the front by first making a stop cut at the thigh. Do this by pressing the blade of your knife down the corner of the thigh. Then, carve toward that stop cut. The rest of the thigh can be carved upwards and doesn't need a stop cut. Put your knife on the line, press down, and rotate the knife as you're cutting, like you're revving a motorbike.

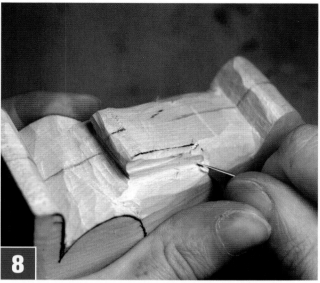

8

Round off the neck and refine the legs. Below the head, make another stop cut and round off the neck. Around the legs, create a smooth transition at the top, making a sort of scooping move with your knife.

9

Copy the pattern onto the bottom of the rabbit and remove the wood between the feet. Do this with a small gouge such as a ¼" (6mm) #8. Work your way from the front to the back. Following the curvature of the belly, you'll end up with a nicely rounded underside.

10

Round off the back, all the way up to the head. Use the pattern of the feet as a guide for the curvature of the back.

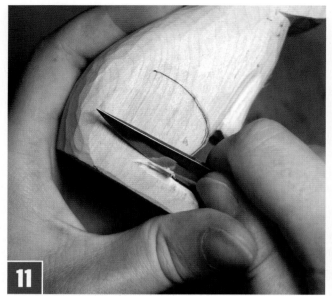

11

Using your knife, make a V-shaped cut, separating the back foot and thigh. Cut down from the top and up from the bottom. When you're doing this, you automatically start rounding off the thigh and feet as well.

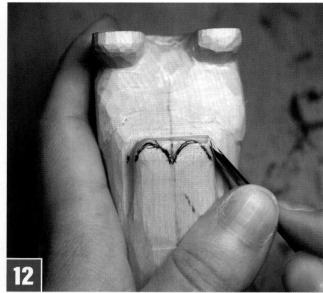

12

Round the feet. Using a small, flat gouge, such as a ¼" (6mm) #6 gouge, round off the front of the feet. For the final bit, use a small V-shaped gouge, such as a ⅛" (3mm) #11.

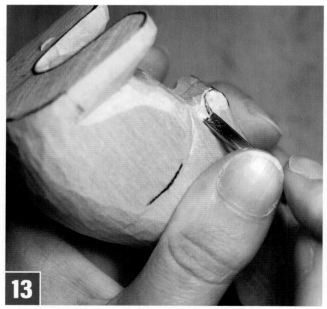

13

Redraw the pattern on the side of the front feet. Use a small gouge, such as a ⅛" (3mm) #11 and a ¹⁄₃₂" (1mm) #11 gouge, and start removing the wood between the foot and stomach. During this process, you'll also remove some wood from the stomach, slimming the rabbit down.

14

Continue carving the front. Using a small, V-shaped gouge, such as a ⅛" (3mm) #11, remove the wood between the two feet. Using the same gouge, carve a ¾" (2cm) long line between the two front legs. You can make this deeper and more pronounced with an even smaller gouge, such as a ¹⁄₃₂" (1mm) #11 gouge. With a very small gouge, like a ¹⁄₃₂" (1mm) #11 gouge, carve a thin line from the armpit down to the bottom of the feet. This will give more depth to the legs. You might have to carve away some more wood down the side after this step. You can now round off the front legs and feet.

Copy the pattern onto the head. Remove the highlighted wood down the side of the head.

Round off the head. When doing this, you want to make sure there is a smooth transition between it and the body.

Copy the pattern onto the front of the ears and remove all the highlighted wood. In between the two ears, this is easiest done with a small gouge such as a ¼" (6mm) #8 gouge and a ⅛" (3mm) #11 gouge. On the outside, you can use your knife.

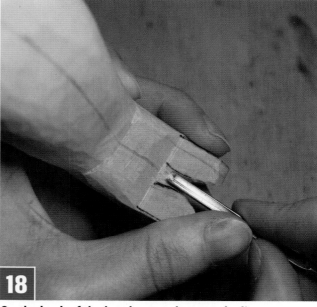

On the back of the head, carve down to the line separating the head and ears. Make sure the rabbit ends up with a round head.

19

Round off the back of the ears with your knife. When doing this, make sure you don't put too much pressure on the ears. While the ears are fairly thick, it'll only take a little too much pressure to make them break.

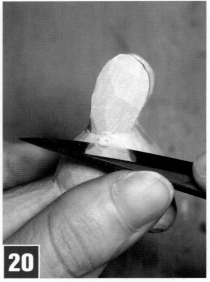

20

Define the ears from the head. On the side of the head, where the ears meet the head, carve away some wood, to create a clear distinction between the ears and the head.

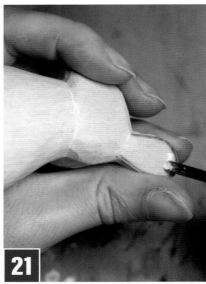

21

Hollow out the ears. Along the outer edge of the ears draw a ¹⁄₃₂" (1mm) line with a pencil. Inside of this line, carve away wood with a small gouge, such as a ⅛" (3mm) #11, to create the hollow inside of the ear. At the top of the ear, make some stop cuts with your gouge. This will prevent you from accidentally slipping and cutting away a small section of the rim of the ear. Don't make the ear too thin.

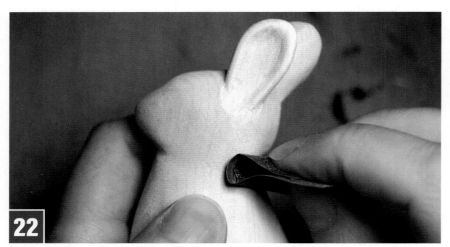

22

Begin sanding. Start sanding with 80 grit to quickly get rid of any large bumps and ridges left over from carving. You can leave the inside of the ears for the next grit. Fold up the 150 grit and sand all over and inside the ears. Once done, move to 320 and sand everything smooth. Then, move to 600 grit. After having finished with 600 grit, hold the rabbit under running water. This will raise the grain and any leftover marks. After letting it dry completely, sand the rabbit again with 600 grit for an extra-smooth finish.

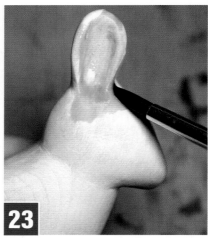

23

Apply a finish. I've used mineral oil, but you can use what you like best. Apply this finish with a cloth or a brush.

Leaping Whale

This was the first sea creature I ever made. Follow these steps and you'll end up with a stylish looking humpback whale. I've been lucky enough to see them in real life once, and they're incredible to encounter in the wild. They're so much bigger than you'd imagine, truly giants of the ocean.

TOOLS AND MATERIALS

- Saw
- Sloyd knife (I use a Morakniv 106)
- Pen/pencil
- A ⅛" (3mm) #11 gouge (I use a Pfeil L 11/3)
- A ¹⁄₃₂" (1mm) #11 gouge (I use a Pfeil L 11/1)
- ⁵⁄₃₂" (4mm) drill bit
- ¹⁄₃₂" (1mm) drill bit
- Drill
- Wire cutters
- Paintbrushes
- Basswood: 2⅛" x 1½" x 7⅞" (5.3 x 4 x 20cm)
- Basswood: ⅜" x ⅝" x 2½" (1 x 1.6 x 6.5cm), times two. These pieces will form the pectoral fins.
- Basswood: 1³⁄₁₆" x 2" x 2¾" (3 x 5 x 7cm). This is the base.
- Wood glue
- Steel round bar: ⁵⁄₃₂" (4mm) thick and 6" (15cm) long. The advantage of using metal is that you can bend the whale in the correct position if the hole you've drilled isn't exactly to your liking.
- Copper wire (x4): ¹⁄₃₂" (1mm) thick, ³⁄₁₆" (5mm) long
- Black watercolor (I use Winsor & Newton Lamp Black)
- White watercolor (I use Winsor & Newton Chinese White)
- Mineral oil

PROJECT PATTERN ON PAGE 133.

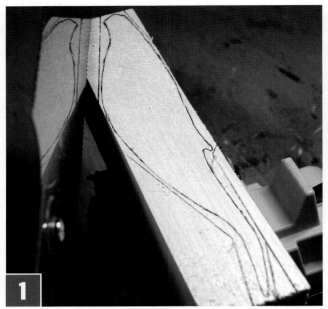

1

Copy and cut out the side view pattern. Make sure the grain runs from the tip of the nose to the tail. Use a saw to cut it out, sawing as close to the lines as possible.

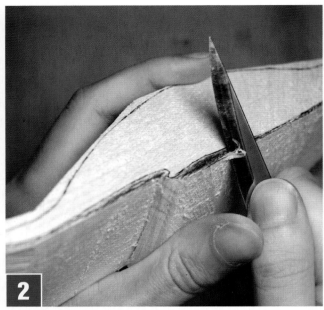

2

Remove all the highlighted wood on the back of the whale. Once you've done this, draw a line down the center of the back.

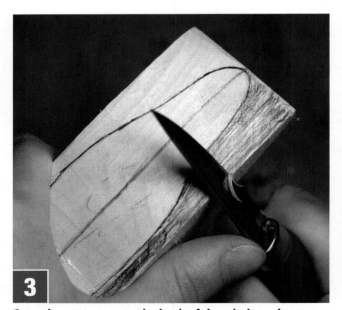

3

Copy the pattern onto the back of the whale and carve. Remove all the highlighted wood on the right side of the whale. This is the side without the main pattern on it.

4

Remove all the highlighted wood on the underside of the whale. Be careful not to thin the tail too much.

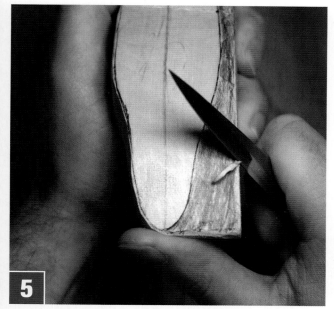

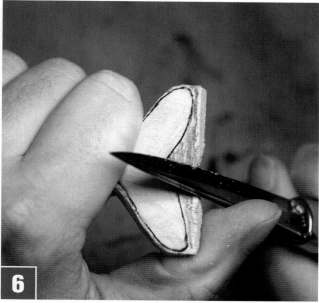

5 **Remove all the highlighted wood on the left side of the whale.** This is the side on which you drew the main pattern at the start of the project.

6 **Remove the material between the tailfins.** Use a series of small cuts here, aiming for symmetry.

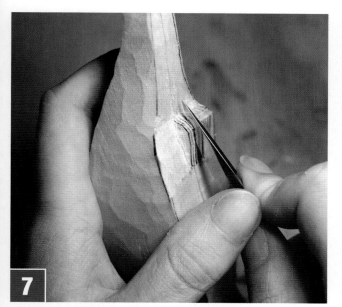

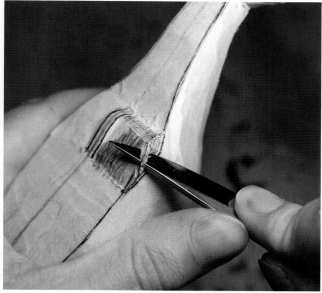

7 **Carve the dorsal fin.** On the side, redraw the pattern below the dorsal fin so you know how far down you have to remove the wood. On the back, make two marks 1⁄16" (2mm) from the center line, making the fin about 5⁄32" (4mm) wide. Then, remove all the highlighted wood on either side of the fin. Right next to the fin, score a line with the tip of your knife. This will let you easily remove the wood next to it. Finally, carve away the rest of the highlighted wood, creating a smooth line running from the front to the back.

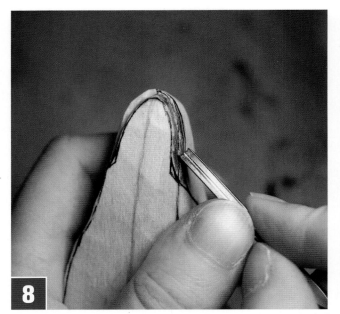

Carve the mouth. Copy the pattern of the mouth onto the left, right, and the top of the whale. With a small gouge, such as a ⅛" (3mm) #11, remove all the highlighted wood. With an even smaller gouge, like a ⅟₃₂" (1mm) #11, carve along the line from the corner of the mouth. You might have to go back to this when you start rounding off the whale in a future step.

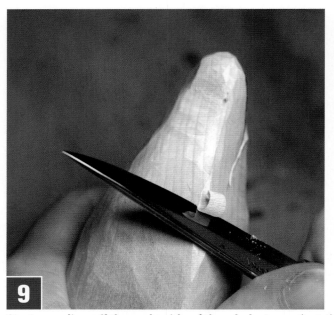

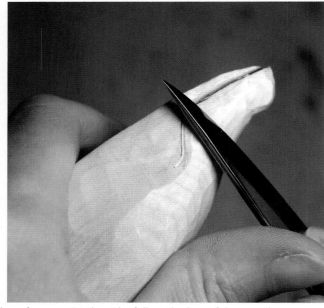

Start rounding off the underside of the whale. Leave the tail alone for now. On the side, follow the line of the mouth.

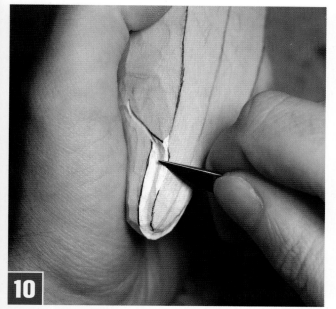

10

Round off the mouth. Start with the top of the mouth. Use the tip of your knife and remove just a small amount of wood, keeping the top quite square. Then, do the same on the bottom jaw, once again keeping it quite square. To make the distinction between the upper and lower jaw even greater, you can carve a thin line between them with a very small gouge, such as a ¹⁄₃₂" (1mm) #11.

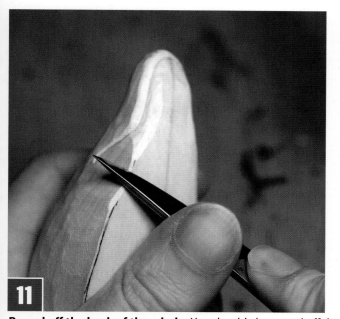
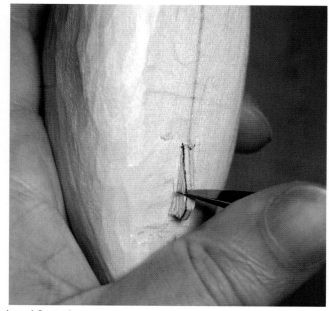

11

Round off the back of the whale. You should also round off the dorsal fin in this step.

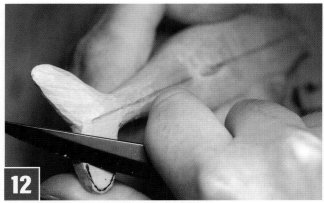

12

Round off the tail. Make the back of the fins thinner than the front. Don't carve them too thin; they might break.

13

Drill a ¾" (2cm) deep hole in the bottom of the whale with a ⁵⁄₃₂" (4mm) drill bit. On the pattern, I've marked at which angle to drill the hole. This will make it appear like the whale is swimming upwards.

14

Begin sanding. Start sanding the whale with 80-grit sandpaper, leaving the mouth for later. With 150 grit, sand the entire whale. This includes the mouth. With this grit, you can also add some more detail to the dorsal fin. Move on to 320 grit, sanding the entire whale, then move on to 600 grit.

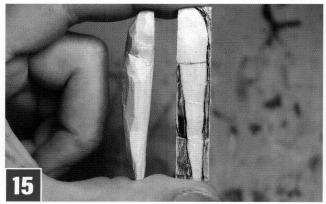

15

Copy the pattern of the pectoral fins onto the piece of wood and cut them out. Make sure the grain is running from the top to the bottom of the fin. Use a saw to cut it out, sawing as close to the lines as possible. Using your knife, round off the edges. Make the fins thinner at the bottom. Leave a completely flat part at the top. This is the part which will be glued to the whale. These should look roughly the same, but some difference is fine.

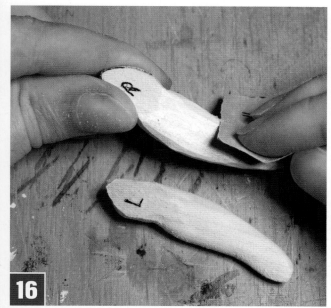

16

Sand the fins. As with the whale, start sanding with 80 grit, slowly working your way through 150, 320, and finishing with 600 grit.

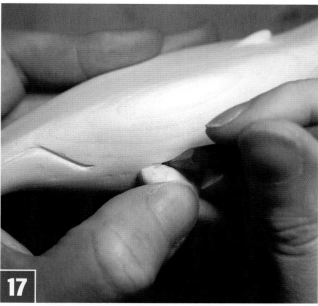

17

Trace the fin joint onto the whale. Holding the fin against the whale, trace a line around the top part of the fin. On the pattern, I've marked where the fin should roughly be. This will mark where the fin is to adjoin the whale.

18

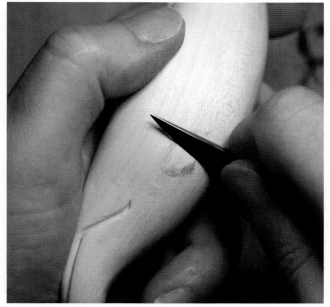

Sand where the fin will adjoin the whale. Color in the outline with pencil, as this will make your process easily visible. With a piece of 150-grit sandpaper glued to a craft stick, sand the area inside the outline completely flat. You can also use your knife and scrape away a tiny bit to make the fin fit to the body. Whichever way you choose, keep checking to see if the fin sits flush against the body. It's all too easy to remove too much wood.

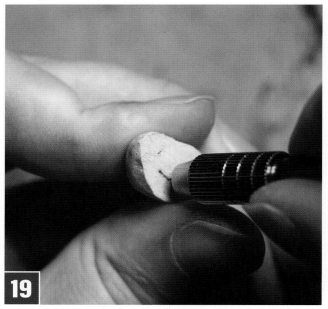

19

Drill two holes into the top part of the fin. Use a ⅟₃₂" (1mm) drill bit. This is the side that sits against the body. The holes should be roughly ³⁄₃₂" (2.5mm) deep.

20

Insert two pieces of ³⁄₁₆" (5mm) long copper wire into the holes. Then, press the fin against the body. This will make a mark exactly where you need to drill the holes in the body. Now drill the holes to the same depth as in the fin. These pieces of wire are there for when you glue the fins to the body, making sure the fins stay in the right position while the glue dries.

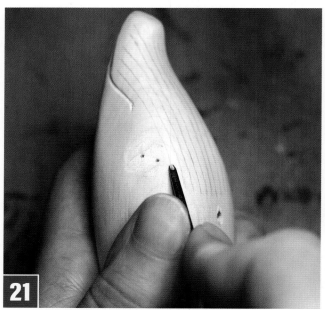

21

On the underside of the whale, draw several lines. Start between the pectoral fins and run up the throat. Thirteen lines is what I have gone for—one in the middle and six on either side of it. Use a very small gouge, such as a ⅟₃₂" (1mm) #11 gouge, to carve away these lines. It's better to carve away a little first, followed by a second pass, rather than trying to carve the entire line in one go.

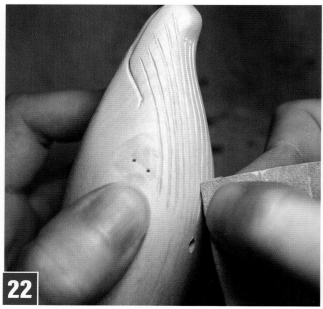

22

Sand away any rough spots that are left, creating a smooth end result. Start sanding with 150 grit, then move through 320 and 600 grits.

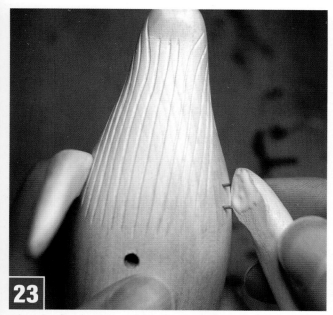

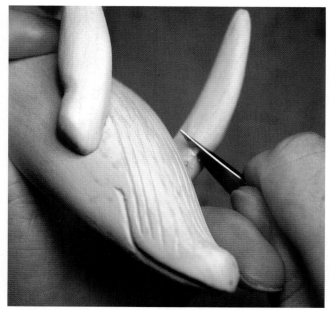

23

Glue the fins in place with a tiny bit of wood glue. Let the glue completely dry before doing any final detailing on the fins.

24

Paint the white parts. Start with the white underside and fins, using a white watercolor (I use Winsor & Newton Chinese White). It might need several coats before you are pleased with the results.

25

Paint the remaining parts of the whale. Use a black watercolor (I use Winsor & Newton Lamp Black). Use a fairly wet brush so some of the paint will bleed into the white parts you painted earlier. This will make a more natural transition between the two parts.

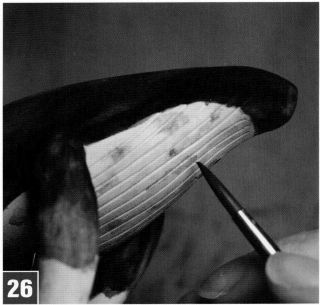

26

Add the spots. Use a very wet brush to add the gray spots on the white fins and underside, representing barnacles growing on the whale. This will make the white less bright and adds a nice touch. With a thin brush, you can add white spots on the head and upper parts of the fin, once again representing barnacles. Don't overdo this. Add a couple, stand back, and have a look. Repeat this until you're happy.

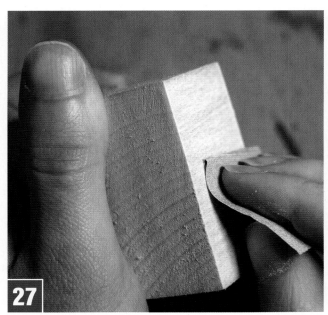

27

Select your base material. For the base the whale will sit on, either cut a piece of wood or use a piece of scrap wood you have lying around. Whatever you use, make sure it is sturdy and the whale won't fall over when it's placed on it. Sand the base with 80-grit sandpaper until you have a smooth finish. Then, sand with 150 grit-sandpaper.

28

Find the center on the top of the base. Do this by drawing two lines on top, connecting the corners. With a ⁵⁄₃₂" (4mm) drill bit, drill a hole in the middle of the base. This should go about ¾" (2cm) into the base. Start off slowly; this will prevent the drill bit from grabbing the wood and splintering it. Try to drill straight down.

29

Complete the base. Sand the base again using 320 grit, getting rid of the pencil marks on the top. Make one final sanding pass with 600 grit for a smooth finish. Insert the metal rod and finish the base. You can oil it, wax it, or paint it.

Patterns

ALL PATTERNS SIZED 100%

Eurasian Wren
Project on page 18

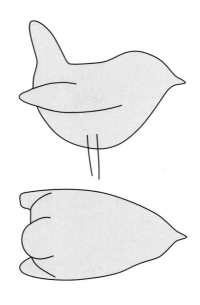

Standing Bunny
Project on page 104

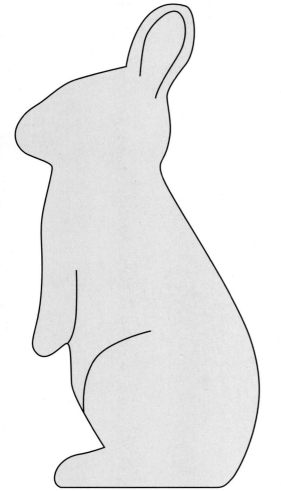

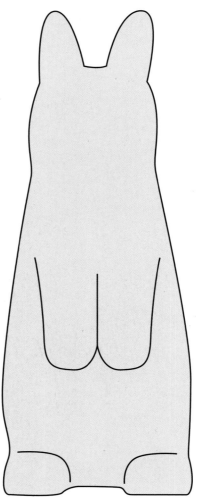

Clucking Chicken
Project on page 23

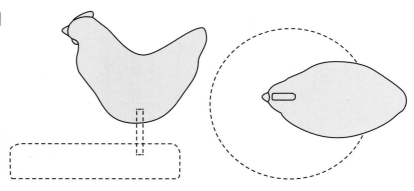

Flying Whooper Swan
Project on page 37

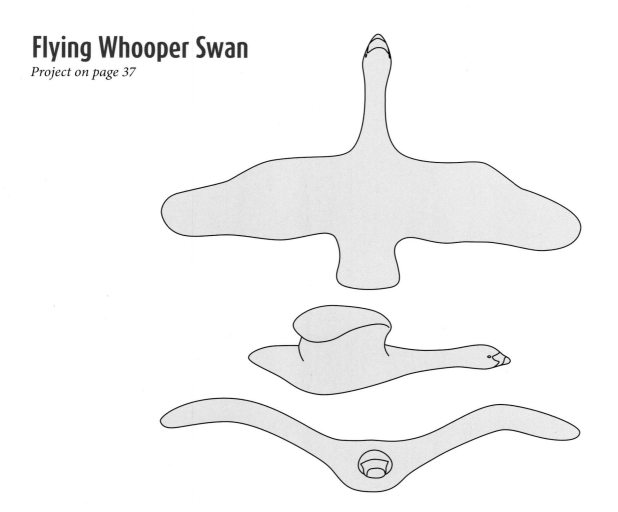

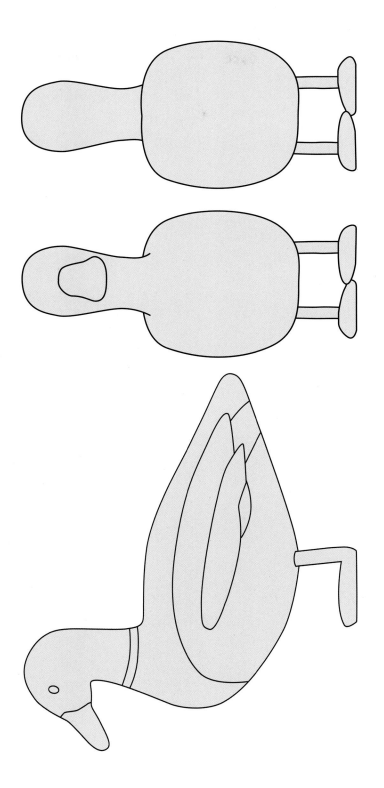

Emperor Penguin

Project on page 44

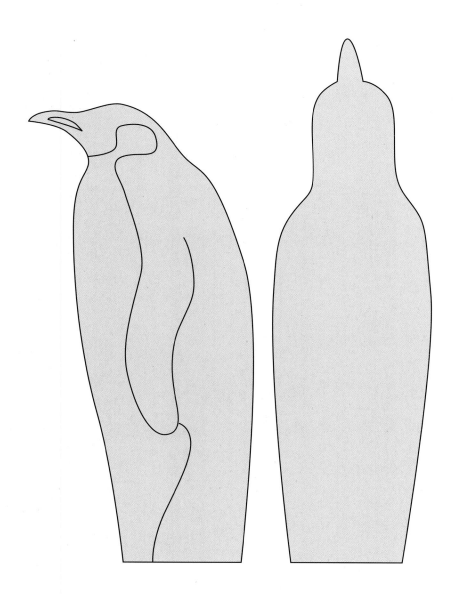

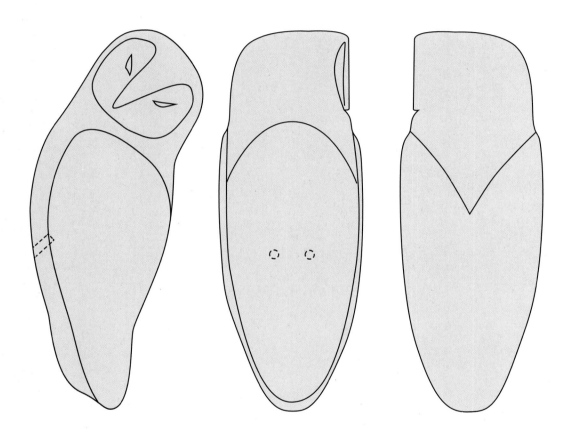

Charging Bull

Project on page 61

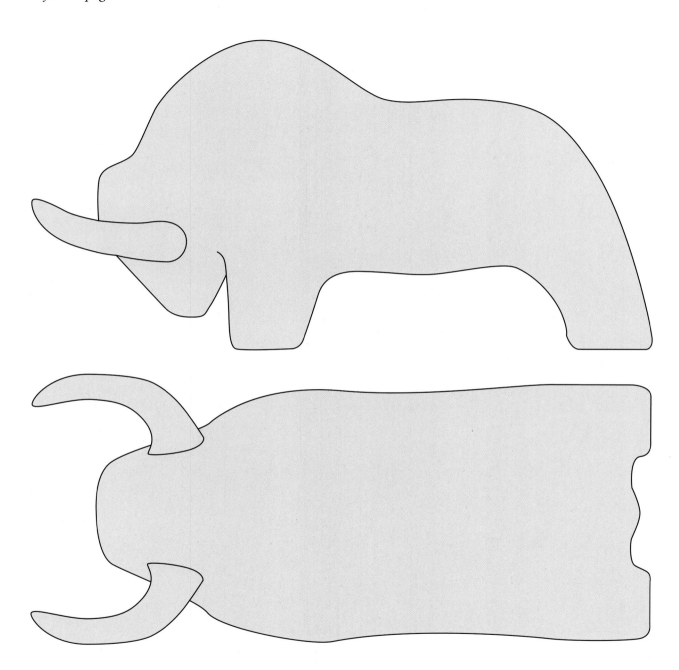

Curious Fox
Project on page 73

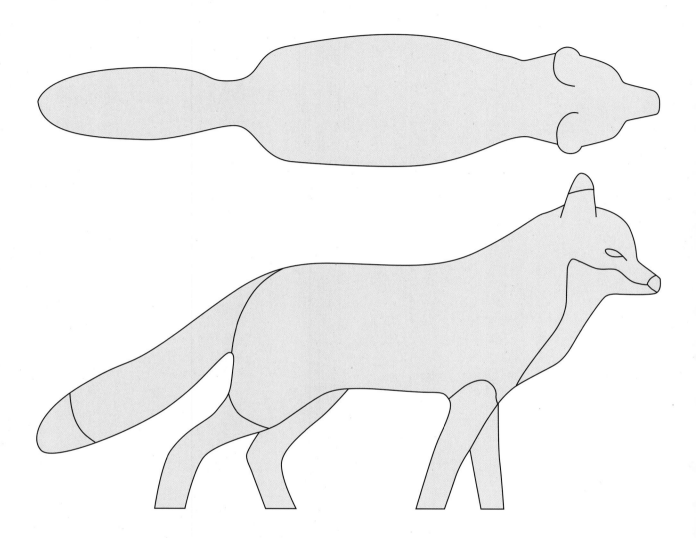

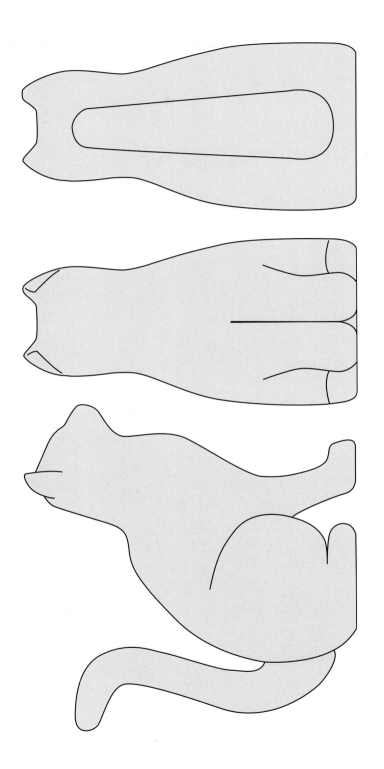

Walking Bear

Project on page 89

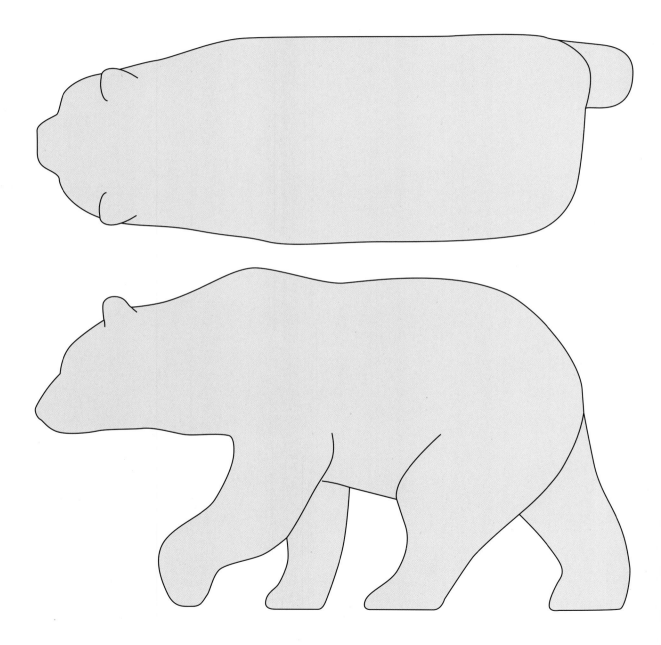

Howling Wolf

Project on page 97

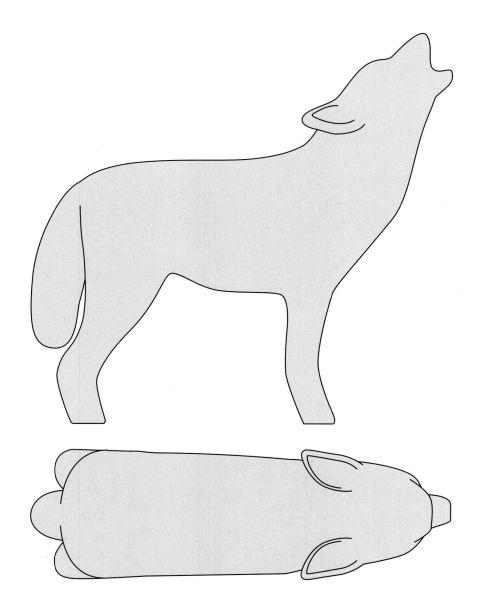

Project on page 111

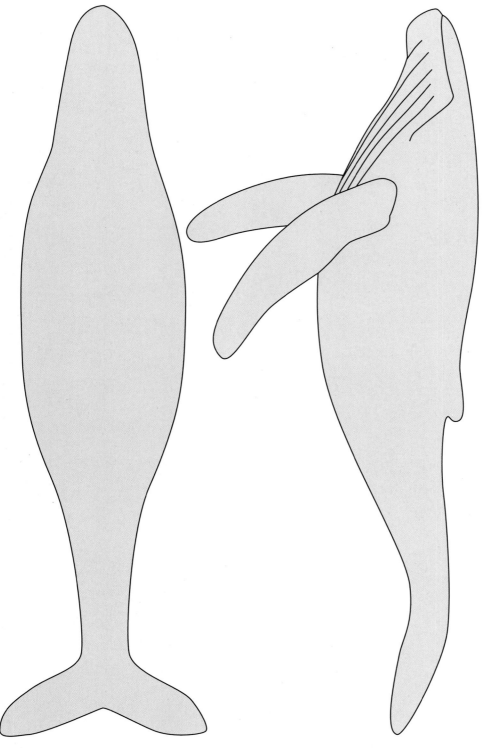

Index

Note: Page numbers in *italics* indicate projects and patterns (in parentheses).

About the Author

I've been carving since early 2019, starting with a spoon carving class while on holiday in Bergen, Norway. After having made a box full of spoons, I wanted to see if I could also carve something else. The bull in this book is based on one of the very first animals I ever made.

My favorite things to carve are small birds. They are easy and quick to make, fun to paint, and a nice thing to give away as a present. There are more than 10,000 species of birds, so I have plenty of inspiration for new birds to make. I live close to the coast, and on my many bike rides (I am Dutch, after all) I often find pieces of driftwood. These, I can use as a nice base for my creations.

In 2022, I had the opportunity to show my work in a small gallery as part of a local art route. It was such a thrill to see how people react to my work in real life. It's very different from posting a photo online and getting a like. I recommend it to anyone, even the introverts among us.

You can find me on Instagram at @WoodByWout and on Etsy under the same name.